The Rubrics Way

Using Multiple Intelligences to Assess Understanding

David Lazear

Zephyr Press

Chicago

The Rubrics Way: Using Multiple Intelligences to Assess Understanding

Grades K–12+

©1998 David Lazear

ISBN 1-56976-087-X

Editor: Stacey Shropshire
Design and production: Daniel Miedaner
Illustrations: Shaun Bailey
Cover design: Joan Sommers Designs

Published by:
An imprint of Chicago Review Press
814 North Franklin Street
Chicago, IL 60610
(800) 232-2187
www.zephyrpress.com

≋ Zephyr Press is a registered trademark of Zephyr Press, Inc.

Library of Congress Cataloging-in-Publication Data
Lazear, David G.
    The rubrics way: using multiple intelligences to assess understanding / David Lazear.
        p. cm.
    Originally published: c1998.
    Includes bibliographical references.
    ISBN 1-56976-087-X (alk. paper)
        Intellect. 2. Intelligence tests. 3. Educational tests and measurements.
    4. Psychological tests. I. Title

    BF431 .L4323 2001
    153.9'3—dc21   2001056908

Contents

Preface

In virtually every multiple intelligence workshop I conduct, the most frequently asked question is "What about assessment?" The question takes many forms because the assessment issue has many faces:

- How can multiple intelligences be used to assess academic progress?
- What should we do about state, local, and national standardized proficiency tests?
- How do we grade MI products? And how do we report this stuff to parents?
- No matter how good MI is, you don't get to paint a picture, sing a song, or do a role-play on the SAT! How can MI be used to prepare students for such tests?
- Will teaching and learning with MI help students get into college?
- Is all this really preparing students to function in the "real world"?
- Why waste time teaching with all the intelligences when I know they're only going to be tested in verbal-linguistic and logical-mathematical ways?
- Shouldn't you be talking to our school board or our legislators? Aren't they the ones making policies that are judging us and our students from a very narrow standpoint?
- MI is exciting for me. Kids like it. It helps them. But how do I find time to use it when most of my time is spent getting students ready for testing?

I naively thought my first book on assessment, *Multiple Intelligence Approaches to Assessment,* had provided at least my answers for every conceivable question on MI and assessment. *I was wrong!* Today I have far more questions than answers. In fact, as contemporary brain-mind research continues to teach us more and more about the brain's neurology and the way it cognitively processes information, I am beginning to feel that there are no final answers to most of the questions listed above. Every so-called answer seems to generate a new set of questions.

If there is a final answer, it may be what the literature is calling "brain-compatible teaching and learning," and the process of school reform, school restructuring, and school renewal based on making schools more brain compatible. We are changing and our schools are changing as we seek to bring them in line with the new information that is coming to us from the frontiers of brain-mind research—research that is presenting exciting new information about what a human being is and what our capacities are. I, for one, am filled with hope for the educational profession today. I cannot think of a better time to be an educator in humankind's long journey than the current one. At the same time, there has probably never been a more frustrating time to be an educator. So much of what we know are best practices (based on current educational research on teaching and learning) and what we know about how the brain learns (and therefore how we should be teaching) are blocked by many school board policies and state-, province-, and local-mandated reforms that are rarely rooted in current education and brain research, nor in the actualities of the state of education today as we rapidly approach the turn of the century.

This book is still another attempt to answer the questions I posed earlier. It is an extension of the work I presented in *Multiple Intelligence Approaches to Assessment;* it looks at ways to create and use MI-based rubrics to enhance, deepen, and reveal understanding.

The more you use multiple intelligences on a regular basis, the more useful you will find this book; many times and in many ways throughout I make the point that instruction and assessment are two sides of a single coin. In other words, profound instruction by its very nature begs to be assessed, for the learner has an intense desire to use the information, demonstrate understanding, and tell others about it. And a truly great and authentic assessment, one that reveals students' understanding, is in and of itself the instructional tool par excellence that we have at our disposal. There is no greater learning than that which occurs when one must perform that learning for others. I suggest that the key to profound instruction and authentic assessment is rubrics—rubrics that genuinely help students further their learning as opposed to those that judge, label, and point out failure.

Allow me to say up front that I am sure every answer I think I am giving will inevitably spawn more and more questions. However, I've decided that's okay. It's all part of the exciting process of human transformation and development.

There are more people I need to thank for their assistance on this book than space allows. Nevertheless, let me mention a few. Major thanks must be given to those teachers who, on very short notice and a tight deadline, provided me with wonderful examples of MI-based assessments from their own classrooms. There is no better testimony to the power of MI and how it can and is changing our schools than this material. My thanks must also be expressed to the staff of Zephyr Press, especially my editors Stacey Shropshire and Veronica Durie for their undying patience with my chronic lateness in getting the manuscript to them. I need to express my appreciation to Shaun Bailey, a new artist, who did the drawings for this book. I am very pleased with his work. Last, but definitely not least, I want to thank my partner Jim Reedy for his continued support, encouragement, and critique of my work.

David G. Lazear
Chicago, Illinois
1998

Be sympathetic with the type of mind that cuts a poor figure in examination. It may be, in the long examination which life sets us, that it comes out in the end in better shape than the glib and ready reproducer, its passion being deeper, its purposes more worthy, its combining power less commonplace, and its total mental output consequently more important.

—William James

— Part 1 —

The Theory

1
Current Evaluation Methods
Exploring the Current Biases _____

In the United States especially, with its focus on quantitative markers and its cult of educational efficiency, there has been a virtual mania for producing tests for every possible social purpose . . . The United States is well on the way to becoming a "complete testing society." We could encapsulate this attitude thus: If something is important, it is worth testing in this way; if it cannot be so tested, then it probably ought not to be valued. Few observers have stopped to consider the domains in which such an approach might not be relevant or optimal.

—Howard Gardner
Multiple Intelligences: The Theory in Practice

How often have you experienced one or more of the following situations?

- A student can draw elaborate pictures that illustrate understanding of certain concepts you are teaching. Yet you can't let her draw in a formal testing situation because you can't establish criteria for a grade.

- You have a discipline problem in the regular classroom. But in music class, this student behaves well. The music teacher never sees any of the behaviors that are so disruptive in your class.

- You spend an inordinate amount of time preparing kids to be successful on standardized, time-efficient district or state proficiency tests that test only verbal-linguistic and logical-mathematical abilities.

- A very likable student has lots of friends and is a good friend to others. In groups he makes sure everyone succeeds, but for some reason he rarely succeeds himself.

- A student consistently demonstrates her understanding in and through various classroom activities, but she can't demonstrate understanding in a formal testing situation.

- You know that standardized tests do not really give an accurate picture of what your students can do and what they really know, yet you're in trouble if your students don't perform well on them.

All these situations are common in classrooms. We know that most of our students are brighter than our assessments of them imply. Every educator has had many experiences with students who understand the material in classroom discussions, who have a good "working knowledge" of the information, who know how to apply it and use it, but who cannot produce it on a written test. Grant Wiggins poses a provocative question about such situations: "Who has really failed when this is the case?" He notes that *the failure in these types of situations is the test*, not the student and not the teacher. Current assessment tools keep us from accurately assessing students' abilities or their understanding of material. So what are the problems with these instruments?

Deficit-Based Assessment

In my first book that deals with assessment (Lazear 1994), I suggest that the number one problem we face in almost all of our approaches to assessment in the Western systems of education is that we approach it from a deficit base. This approach is most prevalent in two areas: ability testing (sometimes called "diagnostic evaluation" or "intelligence testing") and academic evaluations.

Diagnostic Evaluation and the Search for Disabilities

The deficit-based approach to ability assessing is administering often a whole battery of ability tests that, by design, are really hunting for students' "disabilities," their weaknesses, what they can't do. And then, of course, under the guise of

"being able to more adequately provide services" to address the "learning disabilities" we think we have found, we affix labels to students. Thomas Armstrong (1987), noted author and lecturer on multiple intelligences, notes the following about such assessment tools: "It's clear that these assessments do not objectively test a child's ability . . . Learning disability specialists use a 'test until find' approach in their work, where testers administer assessments to a child until they locate a suspected disability—at which point they stop testing and label the child. If they don't locate a disability after two to three tests, they administer up to fifteen or twenty other tests until they either find a disability or exhaust their entire battery. This way of working with children encourages fault-finding and minimizes the chances of discovering strengths and abilities" (30–31).

The logical extension of this kind of deficit testing is the prescription of remedial education programs to help students "overcome" their "deficiencies." But what do we in fact prescribe? More of what they already can't do! In other words, *we remediate at the point of the weakness*. We hammer away at a student's weakness, thinking that somehow we'll be able to drum things into his head. In a recent workshop I conducted on assessment, the participants and I got into a lengthy discussion about remedial education, especially in language arts and math. A participant raised her hand and said, "The way we approach remediation in our schools makes about as much sense as trying to communicate with a person who is totally deaf and prescribing, 'Let's all talk a lot louder'!".

Reread the paragraphs starting with "diagnostic evaluation testing" and consider our approaches to "gifted" education. They are fraught with many of the same problems that occur at the other end of the labeling process. I am not opposed to programs for the gifted and talented, but I have serious questions about *why we don't provide them for all students*. It seems that the students who aren't doing well in the regular classroom are precisely the ones with whom we should be trying different ways of teaching and learning. We also need to do some serious soul searching about what we mean by "gifted." Students qualify to get into most gifted programs by scoring well on various kinds of verbal-linguistic and logical-mathematical tests. There are obviously some students who excel in the so-called "academic" areas and can often handle an accelerated learning push. But why are these students considered more gifted than those who achieve at high levels in so-called "nonacademic" areas?

Academic Evaluation and the Highlighting of Failure

When we look at the deficit-based approach to assessing academic progress, what we see is similar to a rather cruel and frustrating game in which student and teacher are pitted against each other. The goal of the teacher is to devise a test that will clearly show students what they don't know. It often turns into a devious "academic gotcha!" game filled with many surprises, secret codes that only those "truly in the know" will understand, and unexpected twists and turns. On the other side are the students, trying to "out psyche" the teacher and figure out what will be on the test. Once they are in the process of actually taking the test, the game turns into a second-guess-the-teacher game, with students trying to figure out what the teacher wants and will accept as correct answers to various questions. They also often spend their time trying to deceive the teacher by concealing what they don't know. Obviously this description is a bit of a caricature; however, in far too many situations, especially in high schools and colleges, this system is exactly the one used. Think about what students do when you hand a test back to them. Have you ever carefully analyzed their first responses? They look first at the grade, then they look for what they got *wrong*.

Gardner (1993) comes at the issue from the perspective of the psychologist, but his comments could apply as well to teachers and administrators who are involved in various kinds of formal testing: "An equally lamentable aspect of formal testing is the use made of scores. Individuals receive scores, see their percentile ranks, and draw a conclusion about their scholastic, if not their overall, merit. In my own view, psychologists spend far too much time ranking individuals and not nearly enough time helping them. Assessment should be undertaken primarily to aid students. It is incumbent upon the assessor to provide feedback to the students that will be helpful at the present time" (178).

We can also see the power of the deficit-based approach in all forms of so-called "standardized" tests, which many mistakenly assume promote high standards. We expect all students to perform well on these tests in order to graduate. There are several problems with the standardized tests. Grant Wiggins (1992) points out one of these by posing the question, "Have you ever seen a standardized kid?" When we collapse a body of knowledge to fit the kinds of responses one must make on a standardized assessment instrument (for example, short answer, true or false, fill in the blank, multiple choice), we ironically *reduce* the standards to which we are testing. These responses rarely go beyond the lowest level of thinking on any taxonomy of cognitive abilities.

Standardized approaches to academic assessment also tend to lead to the assumption that "the knowledge" and "the learner" are somehow separate entities that can be objectified. In reality, the two are inextricably woven together. Yes, there is an objective body of knowledge, but whether or not it is in fact deeply *known* and *understood* depends on a learner who knows and understands. When we are concerned to assess this knowing and understanding, we must honor this profound, subjective relationship between a student and learning.

Grant Wiggins (1992) elaborates on this relationship by proposing that "There is an inescapable moral dimension . . . to the assessment relationship—a dimension we ignore" (8). He comments on the immorality of these kinds of tests:

> When our sole aim is to measure, the child is invariably treated as an object by any test . . . The educative role of genuine assessment is always at risk if by *test* we mean a process in which we insist upon our questions, our timing, and our imposed constraints on resources and prior access to the questions and in which we see our scoring and reporting needs as paramount. *When we isolate the learner's "knowledge" from the learner's character in a test, we no longer feel an obligation to get to know the assessee well (or even to pursue the meaning of an answer). It is no longer obligatory to worry whether we have provided students with the opportunity to have their achievements thoroughly examined and documented; it is no longer obligatory to construct opportunities for them to show what they can do.* (4; emphasis mine)

The Linguistic-Mathematical Fallacy

Another major problem that seems to be entrenched in all approaches to formal education in the Western world threatens the very fabric of authentic assessment and thus the whole educational enterprise itself. My tentative name for this problem is the "linguistic-mathematical fallacy." In a nutshell, this fallacy assumes that the true, ultimate, and primary measure of one's learning is the ability to express knowledge in a written, logical form and to perform accurate mathematical calculations. Look at several current anecdotal and statistical examples of this fallacy in action.

1. I recently received The National Education Goals Report Summary (1997). (If you are not familiar with these goals, you will find them in the appendix.) At first glance, they seem valid; everyone would probably agree that these are admirable goals. The report contains a "U.S. scorecard," which tells how well U.S. students did in achieving these goals in 1997. The report

is devoted primarily to a discussion of what the United States must do to be first in the world in mathematics and science. Notice the bias in the report's answer to the question, "How can we raise mathematics and science achievement to world-class levels?"

- Set tougher standards in mathematics and science to be comparable to the best in the world.
- Align with the standards in other components of the education system, including curricula, instruction, textbooks, assessments, and school policies.
- Strengthen teachers' subject-matter knowledge and teaching skills in mathematics and science, and move state teacher policies more in line with instructional goals embedded in state standards.

2. The practice of state- or local-level, standardized proficiency testing is on the rise in the United States and Canada. Several questions about these tests must be raised, chief among them being what is actually being tested and how it is being tested. What is the role of these tests in preparing people to assume a responsible, active role in society? The tests focus primarily on verbal and mathematical skills, the "three Rs" we hear so much about. The three Rs are as important as ever, but they alone do not guarantee one's

success in our post-modern, technological, multicultural world! Why don't we have a national forum on what "basics" are needed today and will be needed in the twenty-first century?

In principle, I have no quarrel with proficiency tests per se, but I have a major problem with how they are conducted, how the scores are interpreted and used, and with the narrow and biased range of proficiencies the tests value and purport to be testing.

In *Multiple Intelligence Approaches to Assessment,* I share the work of Emily Grady (1992) on portfolio assessment. One comment bears repeating here: "There seems to be little correlation between testing and producing successful students. American students are among the most tested yet academically deficient in the industrialized world. According to many educators and psychologists—even the head of Education Testing Service—*standardized tests just do not pass muster as a method of improving student performance. In fact they may be undermining the very purpose they were intended to serve*" (6; emphasis mine).

Teachers are implicitly expected to teach to these tests. They know all too well that their performance and the performance of the school itself will ultimately be judged by how well students score.

More frequent and more difficult testing of students as a means to improve our schools simply cannot be empirically documented as a viable strategy. Yet in recent years, parts of U.S. government have been pushing for national testing, which is very much akin to a person whose goal is to lose weight being told to use better, more precise scales and a more rigorous, more frequent weighing program!

3. Lust for time-efficient testing procedures that are easily graded, if not by scantron, then by a simple answer key contribute to the fallacy because we tend to think verbal-linguistic and logical-mathematical stuff is more "objective" than stuff that results from the other intelligences. We also mistakenly believe that everyone understands it. It would be far more difficult (so the argument goes) to have to grade a project that involves painting a mural, for example. In MI assessment workshops I conduct, one of the most frequent comments I get from teachers is "I'm sure there are other ways I could test my students that would be more fair and that would benefit them in their learning, but I just don't have time to create, administer, and grade these kinds of assessments! We see so many students in a day, such assessments just aren't practical!" Instead, we opt for various kinds of verbal-logical short-answer, information recall tests. Wiggins (1997) says the following about such tests: "We have the tests we deserve because we are content to reduce 'assessment' to 'testing' and to see testing as separate from learning—something you do expediently, once, after the teaching is over, to see how students did (usually for other people's benefit, not the student's) . . . It is inevitable that we come to rely on the most simple, efficient, and trivial tasks that can be reliably used. Saving time and labor becomes a paramount design virtue and causes every [test] designer to rely on simple, quickly employed, and reusable (hence 'secure') items" (3).

In other words, we go for the lowest common denominator; namely, assessments that are easy to understand, easy to grade, easy to administer, and easy to compare with other verbal-logical results. While this desire for efficiency may be needed and admirable in certain situations, it can very quickly undermine the very purpose of getting an education, namely, a deep understanding and assimilation of learning to prepare for effective living in the future. Furthermore, it is simply not compatible with the findings of contemporary brain research on how the brain actually operates best and how it learns! Grant Wiggins (1997) says on this point, "The willingness of faculties to machine-score a local test or refer students' answers to a key devised for quick marking during a faculty meeting reveals that teachers, too, not just professional test makers, think that human judgment is an unnecessary extravagance in sound assessment . . . Why have the band director, debate coach, science fair judge, play director, and volleyball coach not succumbed to the same thoughtless or fatalistic expediency? Because they understand that the *"test" or performance is the course, not something you do after it*" (3; emphasis mine).

In workshops a corollary to the time-efficiency objection often comes up: "So, what's it going to take to get and keep a good job? Your boss certainly isn't going to let you sing a song when she wants a report! You can't earn a living based on the other intelligences!" Even though this is a fairly simplistic and somewhat naive objection, I nevertheless find myself responding by pointing out some of the meaningful and productive careers that are in fact within the other intelligence domains. While I do not believe there is a *fait accompli* link between any intelligence and a career, an intelligence strength is a probable indicator of how one will pursue whatever career he or she follows. Read any of the plethora of upper-level management books on the market today; you will rapidly notice several MI motifs that run through these publications. You'll find that employers want people who can be effective members of a team. They want people who are creative thinkers and problem solvers and who can also take their creative ideas and piggyback them with other creative ideas to come up with better and more creative ideas. Employers want employees who are self-reflective, people who can self-evaluate and correct their work. In other words (my words!) employers want people who are able to access all their intelligences, not just the verbal-linguistic and logical-mathematical.

4. College entrance exams test almost solely for and with the verbal-linguistic and logical-mathematical intelligences, even though they supposedly cover all subject areas. And colleges typically rely heavily on these test scores and other math, science, and English grades to determine acceptance into the programs. Parents often say to me, "All this MI stuff is fun and interesting and kids really like it, but will it help them on *the* test? They're not going to be able to do a role-play or paint a mural on the SAT, so why waste time

with this?" Teachers often make a similar comment in MI training workshops: "Yes, we should be using all these MI strategies and tools with kids. I'm sure it would help them with their learning. The problem is, these neat MI things aren't on the test so we can't take much time for them!"

In *Multiple Intelligences: The Theory in Practice,* Gardner (1993) discusses the reality that many students who do quite well on formal, standardized, written tests "often 'psyche out' such tests, scoring well even when their knowledge of the subject matter that is ostensibly being assessed is modest" (168–69). Because they have understood how the test is constructed and what kinds of responses are required, we mistakenly think they understand the material, when really what we have assessed is their ability to take these kinds of tests!

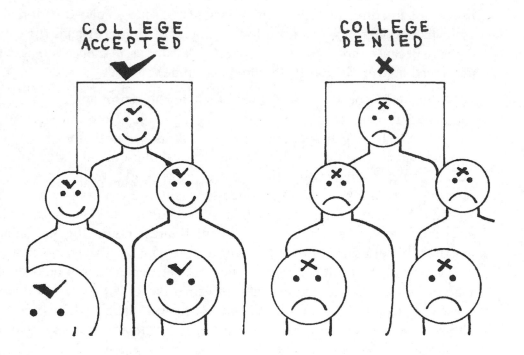

Of course the greatest disservice is when the scores are published in local newspapers, supposedly giving the public an accurate indicator of the "state of education in the nation" and no one seems to question the accuracy of this assumption. In *Multiple Assessments for Multiple Intelligences,* Jim Bellanca, Carolyn Chapman, and Beth Swartz (1994) point out what is most likely the real rationale behind much of the testing that occurs in our schools:

Standardized tests, other than having some predicting value, do little else than please opportunistic politicians and school administrators whose student populations are geared to do well. Seldom are these tests used to determine the defects of the system-imposed learning process. Often [the tests] are used to punish a teacher or principal for not having a class or school 'up to standard' or to force teachers into more rigid adherence to a weak standard. (x)

These tests are perfect examples of the stranglehold the linguistic-mathematical fallacy has on our systems of education. We know nurturing and developing all the intelligences is good for kids—it helps them learn, it boosts their self-esteem, it allows them to become whole people, it helps them respect the wonderful diversity that comprises the human family. Yet, since it's not on the test, we don't mess with it!

In a nutshell, the issues I have been addressing take us to the heart of the majority of assessment problems we face in all Western systems of education: if a student can't write it, read it, talk about it, or compute it, she doesn't understand it. And of course the converse is likewise assumed to be the case: if they can produce the so-called "correct" information on the test, they understand. This assumption is false and naive, and it does a huge disservice to many of the students who inhabit our classrooms daily.

In this chapter, I discuss only the bad news. In spite of my comments, however, I feel *What a great time to be an educator!* Never before has humankind known more about the teaching and learning process than we know right now. The state-of-the-art research that supports our profession is more extensive and more profound than it has ever been. Never have we known more about the human brain and how to teach in ways that are compatible with how human beings actually function. In chapter 2, I turn to the good news—philosophy and classroom practices that are beginning solutions to many of these assessment problems.

2
Effective Evaluation Methods
Exploring the Possibilities

*T*he *"best available knowledge" about how the human brain learns has been knocking at education's door for more than 20 years, yet we have been almighty slow about letting it in. Why? The reasons are numerous but chief among them are . . . the conclusions of current brain research so contradicts traditional educational practices and pictures of how "it's suppos'ta be" that we either ignore the information, misunderstand it, or simply fail to imagine how to implement it.*

—Susan Kovalik and Karen Olsen

How do we move beyond biased assessment practices? Given the way we have structured public education in America, the answer to this question is complex and somewhat convoluted. There is an obvious political answer that must be explored, especially given the highly political nature of school boards and the educational policy making that occurs at state and federal levels. Such is not my primary concern here, however, although I make a few observations about what I think needs to happen.

Part of the answer involves educating the general, tax-paying populace regarding current educational research and why today's schools cannot merely be "the way it was when I was a kid" if we want to prepare today's students for life in the twenty-first century (where, incidentally, they will live most of their lives!). We must undertake a major task—to address the issue Richard Stiggins calls "assessment illiteracy" (1991; see also Lazear 1994, chapter 7); namely, we must take on the task of training the public to be critical consumers of the various assessment data they receive.

Part of the answer involves designing ways to tap students' deep, intrinsic desire to learn and helping them understand the teaching and learning process. Without addressing this issue, no true education is possible, for we will continue to have schools full of students who are merely "playing the game of school" so they can graduate. Playing the game neither serves the needs of society (preparing future citizens) nor the needs of students (equipping them to live effective lives in the future).

It is to this part of the answer I put my efforts in this book. The most effective way to bring about a transformation of our current biased and unfair assessment practices is to implement a multiple intelligence model. In my book *Seven Pathways of Learning* (1993) I address the issue of helping students recognize, appreciate, and understand their multiple intelligences. The research of William Glasser (especially *Control Theory in the Classroom*), Alfie Kohn (especially *Punished by Rewards*), Art Costa, David Perkins, and many others is also very important in helping us develop students who are active, responsible, life-long learners.

Throughout the pages that follow, every time I use the word *assessment*, understand that I mean *instruction-assessment*, for they are really two sides of a single coin. Many of the authenticity difficulties we face today come from the divorce between instruction and assessment. They must be wed again if we are to assess students in authentic ways that genuinely serve the ultimate goals of promoting deep student learning.

Following, I delineate four areas for change based on current research in the cognitive sciences, multiple intelligences, and neuroscience. I present not only the research that calls into question the basic assessment-related assumptions discussed in chapter 1, but more importantly, I suggest practical implications for implementing new approaches to assessment based on MI theory and research—approaches that take us far beyond the existing fallacies, beyond the faddish "latest educational trend or band wagon," and beyond the endless quest for the "quick fix." These suggested areas of change do not relate one-to-one to the problems discussed in chapter 1, for just as the problems themselves overlap and are complex, so the proposed solutions cut across all the problems and are interrelated. Nevertheless, in general, what I have called a multimodal perspective addresses the deficit-based approach to both diagnostic and academic evaluation. The sections "Beyond the Standardized Test," "Beyond the Linguistic-Mathematical Fallacy," and "Beyond Decontextualized Learning" deal with the linguistic-mathematical fallacy and ways to move beyond it.

Beyond Deficit-Based Ability and Academic Testing: A Multimodal Perspective of Assessment

What if, instead of hunting for what students can't do, we had assessments that hunted for the true genius and brilliance in each child? What if our approaches to remediation started with students' strengths and their ability, then used those strengths to help them develop their weaker skills and capabilities? Thomas Armstrong (1987) says, "I prefer not to use the label 'learning disabilities' because people tend to identify too strongly with the term. There's a certain quality of fatalism that accompanies the label—the idea that it's somehow an indelible part of one's learning life rather than something that can be transformed. Instead I like to think of these weaker links as learning difficulties or even learning opportunities because they challenge one to new heights" (30–31). Armstrong even suggests that the "LD" label should be reinterpreted and reunderstood to mean "learning different." I especially like this suggestion, for it is very much in line with contemporary brain research that has shown us that every brain is unique—there are no two brains on the planet that are the same. Yet in our current assessment practices, the written and spoken word is supreme! All students study the same material, are taught in the same way, and are tested in the same way, which implies that all minds are basically the same.

In *Multiple Intelligence Approaches to Assessment* (1994), I expand on Gardner's concept of the creation of intelligence profiles for each student. Through the use of various observation-based instruments, we can indeed gather information on the unique intellectual make-up of individual students, then use this information prescriptively to help them successfully highlight their stronger intelligences. We can then help them use their strengths to work on the development of intelligences that are not as strong.

When it comes to assessing students' academic progress, what if, instead of tests that by design must point out students' failures and inaccuracies, we had tests that provided students with opportunities to show off or demonstrate what they know? What if we had assessments that were a genuine celebration of their learning?

In a district in El Paso, Texas, where I have conducted extensive MI professional development workshops, English literature teacher Mrs. Wieser related the following experience:

It was the end of a major unit on Shakespeare. Throughout the unit, students had been given many opportunities to study and learn the material using multiple intelligences. Mrs. Wieser was continuously teaching students about their many ways of knowing.

It was time for the unit test that the department requires. Mrs. Wieser reviewed the material with the class, making sure all students understood what they were responsible for knowing. Then she said to the class, "Each of you is to figure out the best way you can prove to me that you really understand this material. You may do anything, but you've got to somehow show me that you understand."

As I'm sure you've guessed, some students instantly headed for the essay. However, one young man said, "Mrs. Wieser, I couldn't do an essay if my life depended on it. Could I create a mural?"

Mrs. Wieser said, "Yes, but remember, in and through the mural you must be able to prove to me that you genuinely understand the required material."

Mrs. Wieser told me that this experience changed her life. The young man brought in his mural and rolled it out on the floor. They proceeded to have a four- to five-minute dialogue about the mural in which the young man explained the meanings of various parts of the mural and Mrs. Wieser asked him questions to probe for understanding.

She told me that at the end of the dialogue, she had learned more about his *actual* understanding of Shakespeare than if she had made him write an essay.

Howard Gardner's (1993) quotation really sets the stage for a multimodal approach to assessment:

> The literature on various individual strengths as well as the findings on diverse cognitive styles, has crucial education implications. To begin with, it is important to identify strengths and weaknesses at an early point so that they can become part of educational planning. Striking differences among individuals also call into question whether individuals ought to be taking the same curriculum and whether, to the extent that there is a uniform curriculum, it needs to be presented in the same fashion to all students.

> Formal tests can be an ally to the recognition of different cognitive features, but only if the tests are designed to elicit—rather than mask— these differences . . . *It is particularly important that instruments used in "gatekeeping" niches (like college admissions) be designed to allow students to show their strengths and to perform optimally. Until now, little effort has been made in this regard and tests are more frequently used to point up weaknesses than to designate strengths.* (170; emphasis mine)

In *Multiple Intelligence Approaches to Assessment* (1994), I introduce the concept of multimodal assessments as a means to ensure that all students are given fair ways to demonstrate their understanding of the various subject areas and concepts in the school curriculum. Gardner's research into the theory and process of understanding has led him to suggest that if we are concerned to thoroughly assess students' understanding (as opposed to the mere capacity to recall memorized or previously studied material), we must assess them in at least three different ways. If they can accurately "represent their understanding" in at least three ways, they are very likely approaching expertise in understanding the concepts being assessed. In other words, if they accurately write about material you are assessing, you must also require them to represent their understanding visually through, for example, drawing, sculpting, or painting, and bodily through, for example, dramatic enactment, dance, or physical movement.

In spite of the initially perceived difficulty of creating and administering multimodal assessment instruments, it is obvious how this practice would quickly move us into stronger, more accurate, more fair assessment practices. As I say at the end of chapter 1, just because a student can read it, write it, or articulate it does not mean he really understands. It may simply be an indicator that he is good with words, or he may have been lucky at coming up with and expressing the right answer. The converse is equally true; just because he can't express his understanding in words does not mean he lacks genuine understanding. Addressing this under- standing is where the theory of multiple intelligences is revolutionary!

Beyond the Standardized Test

In current modes of testing, intelligence is viewed as unalterable and unchangeable. We are born with certain "inborn abilities" that develop in a fairly regular, pre- dictable way. Therefore, the same kinds of testing instruments can be employed for all students at all ages and will indicate who knows the material and who doesn't.

More and more institutions of higher education are realizing that a score on a college entrance exam is not necessarily a reliable indicator of how a student will perform in college. Any standardized test, almost by design, must focus on coming up with the right answers from the memory banks of one's educational journey or engaging in accurate computations for relatively decontextualized problems. None of the most popular college entrance exams is concerned with the cognitive processing that went into producing the right answer or the actual problem-solving strategies that were employed. And yet, these are some of the very skills and capacities that make for the most successful college students. Gardner (1993) makes the following provocative comments about the nature of human knowledge: "It is erroneous to conclude that the knowledge required to execute a task resides completely in the mind of a single individual . . . It is too simple to say that an individual either 'has' or 'does not have' the requisite knowledge . . . By focusing on the knowledge that resides within a single mind at a single moment, formal testing may distort, magnify, or grossly underestimate the contributions that an individual can make within a larger social setting" (172–73).

Right answers are temporal; the learning process and the whole process of human growth and development are lifelong. Gardner goes on to suggest that we need to learn to look at human cognition in a very different manner: "It makes sense to think of human cognitive competence as an emerging capacity, one likely to be manifest at the intersection of three different constituents: the 'individual,' with his or her skills, knowledge, and aims; the structure of a 'domain of knowledge,' within which these skills can be aroused; and a

set of institutions and roles—a surround 'field'—which judges when a particular performance is acceptable and when it fails to meet specifications" (173). Of the three constituents Gardner mentions, all need to be present in any viable testing situation, especially those that determine who will get into which college. Current tests, such as the SAT and ACT, access only one of these constituents—the domain of knowledge; and even this is often represented at fairly low levels of the full range of human cognition (according to Bloom's taxonomy).

Close your eyes and, as vividly as you can, visualize the following scene, which is based on the work of Dave and Jan Ulrey (1992), national consultants who specialize in the implementation of developmentally appropriate practices. After each point, pause for a few minutes and allow yourself to dream and to reflect on how current schools would be different if they operated in this way.

You have been mysteriously transported to an educational setting in which people understand that children learn best through active involvement in their learning, regardless of grade level.

▶ The instructional practices these people use address the full range of student needs, including intellectual, social, spiritual, emotional, physical, creative, and aesthetic.

▶ The teachers are acutely aware of their students' various learning styles and intelligences and use this knowledge to develop curriculum and teaching strategies.

▶ The school community values the whole child and focuses on developing strengths.

▶ Children share in learning experiences and activities that stimulate growth and development in all eight intelligences, which are equally valued.

In *Multiple Intelligence Approaches to Assessment* I share some of the Ulreys' work. In a nutshell, they summarize the developmental approach as follows: "Developmental learning recognizes that children grow and develop as a whole, not one dimension at a time or at the same rate in each dimension." Probably the pioneer in a developmental understanding of human beings was Jean Piaget. Basically, Piaget asked us to look at human growth and development as a series of qualitatively different stages through which we pass as we mature. The worldview and perspective of the child is substantially and qualitatively different from that of the adult. In other words, children simply do not see or understand the world in the same way as do adults. This statement sounds fairly obvious; however, we have often treated children as if they were but miniature versions of adults. Piaget challenged this treatment by documenting that the world of the infant or toddler has its own internally consistent knowledge structure that is very different from that of a more mature perspective. Although most developmental psychologists no longer hold to a literal version of Piaget's famous stages (sensorimotor, preoperational, concrete operational, and formal operational), these psychologists are nearly unanimous in their view that we need to take very seriously the child's unique understanding, perspective, cognitive modalities, emotional processing, and all manner of psychophysical functioning.

Another reality of a developmental approach to instruction and assessment is that human development is not a simple, neat, orderly, linear, smooth process. One simply cannot create a set of definitive benchmarks of where one "should" be in development and be fair to the nature of the human animal. Each person is a unique, unrepeatable being who deserves the chance to be treated and evaluated as such. These comments do not mean that developmental indices are irrelevant or wrong. However, my observations lead me to question how we currently use these benchmarks to track children, to label them, and to employ various remediation strategies that do not take into account the many differences that exist among us.

Beyond the Linguistic-Mathematical Fallacy: A Cognitive Perspective of Assessment

In the linguistic-mathematical fallacy, the basics are all that really matter. And what are the basics? As the song says, "reading, and writing, and 'rithmetic." Everything else in the curriculum is handmaiden to these three areas. Subjects such as art, music, drama, and dance are usually referred to as "extra" curricular or as "fluff," and are almost always electives. English, science, and mathematics are sovereign! When budget cuts are required, the fine arts parts of the curriculum are the first to go.

A number of years ago, I was conducting a workshop for parents in a district where I had been doing a fair amount of MI staff development training. At one point in my presentation, a gentleman raised his hand.

"Whatever happened to the three Rs?" he asked. "When are you educators going to get back to the basics so that kids are able to get jobs when they get out of school?"

Another chimed in, "Yeah. Why can't school be the way it was when I was there? It was good enough for me and we didn't have any of this fancy research back then!"

I paused, took three or four deep breaths (to prevent myself from doing something irrational or illegal!), then addressed their concerns with one story and three questions.

The Story

A college friend of mine returned to school to become a medical doctor after several years of practicing law. In his first semester, a professor who taught general medicine walked into the class the first day with a brand new textbook. He said to the class, "There is good news and bad news about this textbook. The good news is, you have in your hands the Western world's best available, state-of-the-art knowledge on general medicine. The bad news is that by the end of this term, more than half of the information in the book will no longer be considered accurate, and I have no idea which half is which!"

Question 1

What really prepares students to live successfully in the world? Learning a bunch of "stuff" (which prepares them for a test) or learning how to learn (which prepares them for life)?

Question 2

What are "the basics" when you think about what today's kids will need to live as effective citizens in the twenty-first century, especially considering such things as computer technology and the increasing multicultural reality of our world?

Question 3

How many of you would take your child to a medical doctor who was still practicing medicine the way it was practiced when you were a kid because "it was good enough for you then"? Why, then, would you not want the very best of current educational research applied to your child's education?

Needless to say, I did not win any popularity contests that evening, but I do believe people went home with some new things to ponder.

When considering what I am calling the "cognitive perspective" of MI approaches to assessment I believe there are at least two dimensions that must be considered: the intelligence itself and the content of the curriculum. Gardner (1993) expresses these two dimensions as follows: "The abilities entailed in an intelligence can be used as a means of acquiring information. Thus individuals may learn through the exploitation of linguistic-mathematical codes, or of kinesthetic or spatial demonstrations, or of interpersonal bonds. Even as various intelligences can be exploited as means of transmission, the actual material to be mastered may itself fall squarely within the domain of a specific intelligence" (172).

Look first at the intelligences as "the means of acquiring information." In my own work with MI theory I like to talk about the intelligences as ways of knowing, which first involves evoking, triggering, awakening, or otherwise tapping into the bioneurological processes of the intelligence in question. In that each intelligence can be more or less localized in the brain, one must properly stimulate various regions of the brain to access the various intelligences.

Each intelligence likewise has a unique core set of capacities or core operations, which, when triggered, produce the knowing that is peculiar to that intelligence. So, for example, when visual-spatial intelligence is stimulated or activated, capacities such as forming mental images, graphic representation, active imagination, and finding one's way in space come to the fore of one's cognitive processes. The knowing that occurs will present itself in and through the media of visual-spatial intelligence, namely, images, shapes, color, texture, design, patterns, pictures, and an acute awareness of and sensitivity to spatial relationships. One of the more exciting parts of the research into the nature and dynamics of human intelligence for me is that these intelligence capacities can be developed, enhanced, even taught at any age and at almost any ability level.

The second dimension deals with the "material to be mastered." Each intelligence is related to and resonates with various content in the external and internal worlds and consequently, with those parts of the school curriculum that deal with this content. The content involves learning subject matter, concepts, and so on that are related to specific intelligences; for example, if someone learns a folk dance or a way to execute a gymnastics routine, the knowledge itself is bodily-kinesthetic, or if someone learns how to raise and train an animal or to create plant hybrids, the knowledge is naturalist. One of the more interesting aspects of working with MI in the classroom is that, in principle, all the intelligences can be brought to bear on the task of learning information that is more or less intelligence specific. So, for example, content that is musical-rhythmic by nature (such as creating appropriate sound effects or background music for a story) could be explored through drawing, painting, or sculpting (visual-spatial intelligence), through moving one's body to the various tones, beats, rhythms, vibrational patterns (bodily-kinesthetic intelligence), or through working with a cooperative group or a partner to develop and enhance one's skills and gain a deeper understanding of the concepts involved (interpersonal intelligence).

When we are involved in assessing students' knowledge and understanding of the required curricular concepts and, thus, their academic progress, I believe that both these dimensions must be very much at the forefront of planning appropriate assessment that will fairly and accurately assess where students are in their learning. On the one hand, you have the content, concepts, and material of the curriculum that students must master to eventually graduate from school; on the other, you must work with the various intelligences to help students acquire and demonstrate understanding of those curricular concepts. We explore the practical "how tos" of working with the content and the intelligences simultaneously in chapters 4 through 6 when I suggest models for creating MI-based rubrics.

In *Multiple Intelligence Approaches to Assessment,* I approach the diagnostic task by suggesting the use of a variety of observation-based instruments designed to evoke students' use of various intelligences. The instruments are all based on and adapted from the early childhood assessment effort called "Project Spectrum," a spin-off of Gardner's research in Harvard's Project Zero. Five observation instruments are suggested: student behavior logs, intelligence skill games, intelligence attention foci, complex problem solving, and inventing. The information from these observations is then plotted on an MI Profile Indicator that identifies the unique arrangement and balance of the various intelligences in students, that is, what makes them "tick" intellectually. I then offer a wide variety of tools that could be incorporated into lessons to help students who exhibit very different profiles, for just as no two brains are the same, no two intellectual profiles are the same. We do a great disservice to students when we treat them as if they are all the same. In fact, in *Multiple Intelligence Approaches to Assessment,* I spend a fair amount of time sharing ways to utilize the intelligence profiles in a prescriptive manner, that is, to design intelligence-based individual education plans (IEPs) for all students, not just the "problem cases."

Beyond Decontextualized Learning: A Contextual Perspective of Assessment

In many current assessment practices, the be all, end all of learning is producing correct answers on the test. Reviewing for the test is a matter of going back over the material and committing to memory what one expects to be on the test. During the test, one must not only recall the information but be able to put it in the words the teacher wants.

Can you guess where the following assessment takes place? The descriptions are adapted from Wiggins (1997):

▶ Assessment challenges are not standardized; in fact, they are by design fully personalized, allowing each student free rein as to topic, format, and style.

▶ The test is never secret; the assessment is centered in students' intellectual interests and the thoughtfulness with which those ideas are pursued.

▶ Students are assessed on how well knowledge and interest are crafted into products and performances of their own design, and no student must earn the right to create projects and works of his own choosing.

▶ The setting for the assessment is mainstream, not alternative; however, the schedule that supports such assessment is out of the ordinary, designed to suit the learner's not the teacher's pace.

▶ Each student is assessed only when ready.

▶ Teacher and students are allies in the assessment process; the teacher is the students' guide through the assessment (not an enemy to be "psyched out").

▶ The assessor is obligated to understand the student's point of view in order to validly assess the student's grasp of things (a far cry from the typical "gotcha!" test).

This scenario occurs daily in most kindergartens and graduate schools throughout North America! Grant Wiggins (1997) provides an apt context in which to consider the cognitive perspective in moving beyond decontextualized learning: "At both ends of the school career, we deemphasize one-shot, uniform testing in favor of a careful assessment, from different perspectives, of the student's own projects. We focus more on the student's ability to extend or play with ideas than on the correctness of answers to generic questions. Each piece of work, be it a drawing or a dissertation, is examined—often through dialogue—for what it reveals about the learner's habits of mind and ability to create meaning, not his or her 'knowledge' of 'facts.' At the beginning and end of formal education, *we understand that intellectual accomplishment is best judged through a 'subjective' but rigorous interaction of mind and mind*" (2; emphasis mine).

Unfortunately, the reality is far different in the years between. Standardized and short-answer tests dominate. Students' ability to produce correct answers is valued more than their ability to integrate, synthesize, and transfer knowledge. And, again using Grant Wiggins's words (1997), "They are allowed one attempt at a test that they know nothing about until they begin taking it. For their efforts, they receive—and are judged by—a single numerical score that tells them little about their current level of progress and gives them no help in improving" (2). The result of what I have been describing here has led researchers Lauren and Daniel Resnick, heads of the New Standards Project, to reflect that American students are the "most tested but least examined" in the world.

To move us beyond this situation, we must pursue three new directions: (1) assessment must occur in context, that is, in a real-life situation where students are facing real-life challenges; (2) the assessor and the assessee must focus on deep understanding of the concepts being assessed rather than the assessee's capacity to spit back memorized information; and (3) assessment must be performance based so that students are given feedback on their performance and opportunities to improve. Consider each of these in its own right.

Assessment in Context

A friend of mine did very poorly at math when he was in school; in fact he almost didn't graduate with the rest of us because of his low math scores. Today he is a nuclear engineer who heads a department at a major nuclear power plant in the eastern part of the United States. Can you guess what comprises about 95 percent of his normal daily activities? Precisely the math he could not perform in school. But take that same math and put it in a real-life situation and he can perform at astonishingly high levels. Howard Gardner (1993) summarizes a revealing study in this regard: "It has been shown that experts often fail on 'formal' measures of their calculating or reasoning capacities but can be shown to exhibit precisely those same skills in the course of their ordinary work . . . In such cases, it is not the person who has failed but rather the measurement instrument which purported to document the person's level of competence" (2).

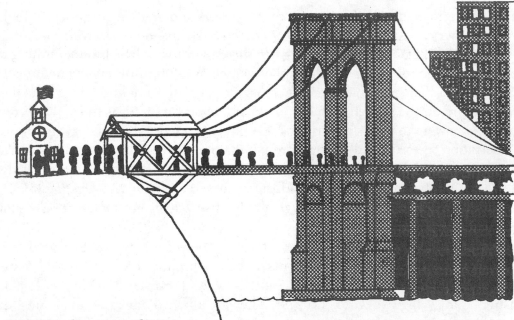

Deep Understanding

An assessment should give us and students information about their grasp and comprehension of the material being learned. What constitutes genuine understanding? Let me cite several perspectives on this crucial question, then make a couple of my own observations.

Campbell et al. (1992) summarize some of David Perkins's research in *Teaching and Learning through Multiple Intelligences*: "When a person knows something, such a statement usually means he or she has mentally stored information and can readily retrieve it. By contrast, when a student is said to understand something, it is assumed her skills surpass stored information . . . understanding refers to what individuals can do with information, rather than what they have . . . When students understand something, they can be observed explaining concepts in their own words, using it in new contexts, making fresh analogies and generalizations and other stretching activities. *Memorization and recitation are not indicative of understanding* (194; emphasis mine).

In *The Unschooled Mind*, Gardner (1991) argues that an individual genuinely understands only when he is able to appropriately apply various knowledge, concepts, materials, or skills (usually initially acquired in some kind of formal or informal educational setting) to a new situation, a new setting, or a heretofore not encountered set of circumstances. He implies that if someone cannot apply the supposed learned knowledge, concepts, materials, or skills in a new situation, he does not really understand. In class, students often appear as if they understand because they are able to furnish back to their instructors the factual and rule-governed information that they have committed to memory. But once out on their own, once expected to figure out which school-learned concepts, facts, or skills are actually applicable to a new situation, they show themselves to be incapable of understanding—and again, often mired at the same level as the proverbial five-year-old.

Finally, as a definition of understanding, one cannot forget Benjamin Bloom's famous taxonomy, which moves from a learning of the "facts, ma'am, nothing but the facts" at the lowest level of thinking, to an awareness and understanding of the process, dynamical relationships, and connections between those facts and the higher-order ability to integrate, synthesize, and use the facts and processes from the previous levels in her regular, daily living.

Rarely do standardized tests or any short answer or multiple choice test move beyond the "facts, ma'am, nothing but the facts." If we are interested in true understanding of our students' learning we must devise assessments from the higher-order realms of thinking—assessments that require students to apply their so-called knowledge to solving problems or creating products in real-world, real-life situations. If they can do so, they understand.

Performance Based

The final aspect of the contextual perspective of assessment is that it should be performance based. The importance of performance-based assessment is powerfully illustrated in Wiggins's words (1997):

> What really counts as evidence of "knowledge"? What is it that we want students to be able to do as a result of schooling? The *de facto* answer, if we examine tests, is that the students must recognize or plug in correct facts or principles to atomistic questions simplified of their natural messiness by the test maker . . . What matters in education is understanding and the habits of mind that a student becomes

disposed to use. Conventional testing cannot tell us . . . what we need to know . . . The problem is clearer still if we ask what counts as evidence that the student understands what was taught. A one-shot, secure test in which the student is required neither to produce a work-product nor to engage in discussion is unlikely to tell us whether the student has understanding or not. Correct answers can hide misunderstanding; incorrect answers, without an opportunity to explain oneself, can easily hide deeper insight. (9)

Elsewhere in his writing, Wiggins suggests several performance-based assessment models currently used, valued, and understood in the larger society that we should be trying to emulate as we design assessments for school. Think for a moment about any sport. Obviously the "assessment" in this case is the actual competition. The main job of the coach is to prepare the team to be successful in the game; in other words, she literally "teaches to the test"! But of course, here you have an authentic test.

Other examples of instruction and assessment being one would include any performing art. Again, the assessment is the performance itself: the drama, the concert, the recital, the ballet. Or consider the visual arts where the assessment is the actual painting, drawing, sculpture, and so on.

I often hear an objection to multiple intelligences that says the approaches I suggest to instruction and assessment will "dumb down" the curriculum, that is, make the material presented more basic to accommodate slower learners. The implication is that one would offer other modes of assessment only because some students know less or are less capable, as reflected in traditional testing. The objection also implies that average or better-than-average students must slow down, which sacrifices their education needs to those who require more help. I have heard the term used in reference to many new approaches to education, suggesting that any attempt to accommodate all learners is dumbing down.

However, I suggest that *what dumb down the curriculum are approaches to assessment that ask students to simply mouth back to the teacher information that was imparted in a lecture or read in a textbook.* Many students are very skilled at the "memorize and recall" approach to school but they have little understanding of the facts, figures, and concepts they supposedly have learned. *What dumb down the curriculum are all forms (both overt and covert) of norm-referenced assessment.* Norm-referenced assessments require the tester to decide, consciously or unconsciously, that not all students can be successful. I was appalled by a recent conversation I had with a teacher in a workshop. Her principal told her that she had given too many As and Bs during a recent grading period. She argued that no one was given a mark that was not earned given the established standards of performance. Nonetheless, she was told to go back and change the grades so they fell more along the lines of the normal (?) curve.

What dumbs down the curriculum are any and all forms of standardization that boil academic achievement expectations down to a set of time-efficient, cost-saving, easy-to-administer tests on which students are given a numerical grade with no real feedback, no suggestions for improvement, and no opportunity to modify their work. Wiggins (1997) makes the following important observations about standards (*not* standardization):

- Standards are never the result of imposed standardization.
- Standards, like good assessment, are contextual.
- Standards relate to jobs done well by individuals (judged within a context of particular purpose and effect).
- Standards are not fixed or generic.
- Standards vary with a performer's aspirations and purpose.
- Raising performance standards requires not standardization of expectation, but heightened demands for quality work from each student in each course. (282–83)

What dumbs down the curriculum is the assumption that the only valid, reliable form of assessment is the formal, written test. The very "discovery" of the plural, multidimensional nature of human intelligence has disclosed that there are many ways of knowing, many ways we acquire knowledge, process information, learn, understand, and know what we know. The bias of the linguistic-mathematical fallacy that has singled out two of these as the only ones that are ultimately valid involves a rather crass implication that education should not deal with the whole person but only those parts that are easily quantifiable.

What dumbs down the curriculum is the failure to recognize and fully utilize the unique gifts of individual students simply because they learn, understand, and know in different ways. The subtlety (and almost unconscious nature) of this approach often reveals itself in teachers' conversations about "the bright kids," who, of course, are those gifted in the intelligences most valued in our schools.

In the remainder of this book I turn to the practical task of assessing students' educational progress using multiple intelligences. The main focus is various models for creating rubrics or criteria to ensure that students are thoroughly examined and that we are gaining a more accurate, more fair picture of their educational progress than if we look only through the lenses of verbal-linguistic and logical-mathematical intelligences.

3
Making the Case for MI Rubrics
What Are They and Why Are They Important?

When we ask, "What motivates the student to perform in school?" we often forget that the most significant motivating force is the student's discovery of his or her capacity to do successful and good work. How one determines whether a student is doing successful and good work should be a collaborative process of standard setting.

—Bena Kalik
"Evaluation: A Collaborative Process"

In chapter 2 of this book I related the story of a teacher in El Paso, Texas, who assessed a student's knowledge of Shakespeare through the student's mural. In a workshop I was conducting last summer a huge controversy broke out over whether or not you can assess a mural. Comments ranged from "You can't judge someone's art work!" to "Assessing what someone has drawn or painted is purely subjective!" to "Fine, they did a nice mural. But how do I know if they really understand?"

Why do we feel we can assess a student's written work but not a student's artistic work? The answer is that we have a clear set of rubrics for the essay.

In *Multiple Assessments for Multiple Intelligences,* James Bellanca, Carolyn Chapman, and Beth Swartz (1994) define a *rubric* as "a rule or guideline that outlines the criteria and indicators of success. The indicators are observable measurable behaviors which show to what degree the student is using knowledge and skill. The criteria are benchmarks which tell to what degree the students are attaining the standard . . . A *standard* is . . . used to measure quantity and quality. The standard is considered to be a reliable and authoritative norm that indicates what is best" (1–2).

Rubrics are a regular part of everyday living. Think about dining at a restaurant and figuring out how much tip to leave your server. The standard in most parts of North America today is 15 percent. However, I have an informal rubric by which I judge the service and decide how much to leave, given the 15 percent standard. If the service is outstanding I usually leave 20 percent. How do I decide? I use my "outstanding service questions" to form an informal rubric:

1. When I need something, do I have to hunt for the server?
2. Is the service attentive (for example, when the rolls are gone, are new ones offered without my having to ask)?
3. Are any issues or problems handled cheerfully and quickly?
4. If the server has served me in this restaurant in the recent past, does he or she recognize me?
5. Is the service friendly without being intrusive?

Now, I'm not suggesting this is a right rubric or one you should use. I am simply illustrating that rubrics are a major part of our lives. **Some rubrics we create and apply to other people and situations**: What are your rubrics for deciding whom your teenage daughter can date? Whom you want as part of your circle of friends? What clothes you want in your wardrobe? **Some rubrics are created by others and applied to us and our situations**: think for a moment about the rubrics for such things as maintaining a good credit rating, passing a driving test, or worshipping in a religious service.

Many teachers tend to steer away from performance assessment because "they take too long to prepare and are too subjective when it comes to grading." However, an essay is a performance task, and we assess essays all the time. How does an essay compare to other kinds of performance assessments? My answer is that *they are basically the same*. In an essay, we ask students to use the verbal-linguistic intelligence to perform. The structure or form is the essay; the "knowing modality" is words, phrases, grammar, syntax, metaphor, simile, idiom, and so on—all the "stuff" of using the verbal-linguistic intelligence to acquire knowledge, process information, understand, and learn. It is probably the sheer familiarity and frequency of designing and grading written work that draws many to these kinds of assessments and makes us feel they are so much easier to create and grade. However, developing assessments for other types of performances is really not as difficult as it might seem. In *Education Update,* ASCD (1995a) quotes and summarizes what Grant Wiggins has said: "Grant Wiggins . . . recommends designing curriculum 'backward from the assessment tasks—deciding what students should be able to demonstrate they know and can do before deciding what to teach them.' Such an approach lends coherence to the entire curriculum. He wrote . . . 'With clarity about the intended performances and results, teachers will have a set of criteria for ordering content, reducing aimless 'coverage,' and adjusting instruction en route; and students will be able to grasp their priorities from day one'" (1, 4). Such an approach to rubrics is developed in this book.

Rubrics in the Classroom
Helping Teachers Evaluate Performance

In *How to Assess Thoughtful Outcomes,* Kay Burke (1994) says, "The key to effective performance is setting the standards and criteria in advance. 'In the absence of criteria, assessment tasks remain just that, tasks or instructional activities. Perhaps most important, scoring criteria make public what is being judged and, in many cases, the standards for acceptable performance. Thus, criteria communicate your goals and achievement standards' (Herman, Aschbacher, and Winders 1992, 44). A rubric refers to the scoring form that contains the criteria to be judged" (x). I suggest that, *without well-defined, clear rubrics, students' understanding will not be discernible*. Several examples illustrate this phenomenon.

- As viewers, we might watch an Olympic athlete's performance and be awed by what we see. Yet when we are told the rubrics the judges are using, suddenly *we see a lot more in the performance* and probably have a deeper appreciation for what we are viewing.

- This past year I attended the opening of a new fine dining establishment in the Chicago area. I was delighted with almost every aspect of the experience. Later, I took a good friend of mine who is an aspiring chef to the same restaurant. He also loved the food. As we ate he gave me a running commentary on what I was eating—how it had been prepared, how the various seasonings were used, how the meal was presented, and so on. Throughout the meal, because of this exposure to the rubrics for preparing and presenting a really fine meal, my appreciation for the whole experience was enhanced significantly.

■ A number of years ago I was living in Korea teaching at an English-immersion language school for adolescents and young adults. One of the learning activities we employed was a real-life simulation in which only English was allowed. In the morning we would work to prepare students for the simulation with the vocabulary words, phrases, idioms, and so on that they would need. The rubrics for the simulation were informal and were determined by such things as the number of complete sentences, incorporating with a certain frequency the vocabulary, grammar, syntax, and so forth into the experience. The simulations were set to push students to make themselves understood as well as to go beyond a mere robotic "mouthing back" of what they had learned in classroom work. One of the most unforgettable of these was a department store simulation. One student who had been having a lot of trouble in the formal classroom organized a robbery of the department store—in perfect English using vocabulary, phrases, and idioms that none of us thought he was getting or understanding. Perhaps the performance aspect of the assessment inspired this "below-average" student to work harder; perhaps he was simply strong in bodily-kinesthetic intelligence, so the performance was a more comfortable means of expression than a written work. Regardless of the cause of his success, the experience reinforced my belief in performance as an accurate, thorough, fair illustration of what students truly know and understand. The rubrics also helped us see things in this student we had never noticed before and gave us criteria through which we could formally assess the student's understanding.

If well-defined rubrics can make visible the depth of students' understanding, fuzzy rubrics or rubrics that are too narrow can hide a student's true understanding. In a workshop I was conducting on the East Coast last year, a high school physics teacher told me about an experience in one of his classes. They had been studying the concept of infinity. One day he decided to conduct a random oral quiz to check for students' understanding of some related concepts. He called on one young man and asked him to explain infinity. The young man said, "Cream of Wheat!" Of course, the whole class broke out in laughter, and the teacher moved on to seek other, more traditional answers that were from the book or his lecture, assuming the student was trying to show off and entertain the class. After class, the young man came to the teacher and said, "I wasn't being a Smart Alec! Don't you understand my answer?" The teacher said, "Please enlighten me!" "Have you ever looked at a box of Cream of Wheat? The picture is of a man holding a box of Cream of Wheat, which has another picture of a man holding a box of Cream of Wheat, which has another picture of a man holding a box of Cream of Wheat." The young man said, "That's infinity!"

The teacher was stunned, for due to an unconscious, narrow rubric, he almost missed a student's genuine insight and understanding.

Helping Students Succeed

Rubrics are also a key to helping students become active, responsible learners. Rubrics must be clearly stated up front so that all students have a picture of what a successful performance would be. Rubrics can also be a means to help students move to new levels of understanding. Rubrics can give students goals to shoot for. Bena Kalick (1989) discusses some of the problems and possibilities inherent in this task:

> "Did I get this right?" "Is this what you had in mind?" "Is this work good enough?" So much of a student's sense of "good" work depends on someone else telling us if we have it right. I am not talking about the kind of work for which there is a single right answer. I'm talking about work that requires complex thinking, problem solving, divergent ideas, and a new synthesis of one's knowledge base, or applying knowledge through performance—the kind of answers that require the students to be the producers of knowledge rather than the reproducers of knowledge. When we move into that zone of uncertainty in which right and wrong are a matter of a shared understanding of expectations and criteria, we need response. We need a mirror placed before our work that provides an opportunity for reflection and constructive criticism for improvement. We need to be provided with an opportunity to talk about our work with others. (313)

If multiple intelligence approaches to assessment are to be accepted and understood, we must have a clear set of rubrics or criteria by which we judge students' performance in the various intelligence areas. As Gardner said, if we are concerned with thoroughly assessing students' grasp and comprehension of the material, concepts, facts, and figures we are teaching, we should require them to represent the information in at least three ways. I cannot state it enough: just because a student can successfully verbalize a fact does not mean she deeply understands. And just because she cannot successfully verbalize it does not mean she doesn't understand.

I do not suggest that students' verbal-linguistic and logical-mathematical abilities should be played down. However, ability in these areas is not the be all, end all of learning. If you require multiple representations on an assessment task, of course, one of the representations could very well be verbal-linguistic or logical-mathematical, but be careful not to let the bias of the linguistic-mathematical fallacy cloud your evaluation here. Verbal-linguistic or logical-mathematical representations are no better or worse than any other kind of representation if the concern is thorough assessment of students' understanding.

The Need for Double Rubrics

Let's look more directly at the task of creating MI-based rubrics to help students make their understanding visible. We are faced with a very interesting challenge: in principle, a student could write a fine paragraph or essay—one that is perfect in terms of the rubrics for a good piece of written work, but the substance of the writing could be thin or the facts inaccurate. The converse is also true. Students' writing could be very basic, with many grammatical errors, dozens of misspelled words, and syntactically awkward sentences; they nevertheless genuinely communicate their deep understanding. When we create and use MI rubrics, we need to operate from a double set of rubrics. Consciously or unconsciously, we already have two sets: One set relates to the curriculum, namely, the information, content, concepts, and material that students must master. The second set of rubrics relates to students' performance and the quality of the product, how well they write the essay, for example (see table 3-1).

MI-Based Assessment Instruments

Howard Gardner (1985) discusses the criteria he uses to identify an intelligence. One criterion is an intelligence must have its own "symbolic notation system": "Much of human representation and communication of knowledge takes place via symbol systems—culturally contrived systems of meaning which capture important forms of information. Language, picturing, mathematics are but three of the symbol systems that have become important the world over for human survival and human productivity . . . While it may be possible for an intelligence to proceed without its own special symbol system, or without some other culturally devised arena, a primary characteristic of human intelligence may well be its 'natural' gravitation toward embodiment in a symbolic system" (66). Gardner also comments that it is unlikely an intelligence's knowledge can be transmitted unless it can be encoded in symbols.

I find the encoding system to be one of the most interesting and challenging aspects of working with multiple intelligences. In *Eight Ways of Knowing* (1999a) I explain the "symbolic notation system" by saying that each intelligence has its own language, jargon, and vernacular. Each also has its own distinct *modus operandi*.

Table 3-1: Double Rubrics: The Curriculum and Intelligence

	Content and Curriculum	Intelligence Emphasis
Instructional Goal and Benefit	To think through your desired assessment objectives and outcomes, and keep them in focus	To encourage the development of students' cognitive capacity in each intelligence
Assessment Focus	To highlight students' understanding of the required material (concepts, principles, facts, figures, and so on)	To encourage students to perform using the capacities, tools, and media of the target intelligences
Teacher's Responsibility	To design assessments that allow students to demonstrate their understanding	To prepare students to show their understanding using specific tools for the various intelligences
Students' Responsibility	To master the required material and to prove thorough understanding	To perform at as high a cognitive level as possible using the specified intelligences

If you really want to understand and work effectively within a given intelligence, you must immerse yourself in its operating mode and learn its language, much like when you visit a foreign country; you'll have a much better time if you in fact speak the language! Part of the difficulty of working with multiple intelligences from an instructional-assessment point of view is that, other than the verbal-linguistic intelligence, their encoding systems, for the most part, are not verbal. They use other media than the spoken, written, or read word:

 The language of the **visual-spatial intelligence** is shapes, images, patterns, designs, color, textures, pictures, symbols, and "inner seeing" that involves such things as active imagination, pretending, visualization, sense of direction, and spatial relationships.

 The language of the **bodily-kinesthetic intelligence** is physical movement and involves such things as creative and interpretive dance, drama, mime, role-play, gesture, body language, facial expression, posture, physical games, and physical exercise.

 The language of the **musical-rhythmic intelligence** (or what I have started to call the "auditory-vibrational" intelligence) is tones, resonance, beats, vibrational patterns, timbre, pitch, rhythms, sounds, including sounds from the environment, humanly produced sounds, sounds from machines, and sounds from musical and percussion instruments.

 The language of the **interpersonal intelligence** is human relating, collaboration, being a good teammate, cooperation, noticing distinctions among other persons, setting common goals, reaching consensus, feeling empathy, and having meaningful encounters with others.

 The language of the **intrapersonal intelligence** is introspection and awareness of internal aspects of the self, including awareness of one's feelings, intuitions, thinking processes, "who am I?" quests, spiritual pursuits, beliefs, and values.

 The language of the **naturalist intelligence** is natural patterns, flora, fauna, species groupings, subspecies categorizations, external and internal sensory experience of the natural world, and all manner of encounters with plants, animals, weather, inorganic matter from the microscopic world to what can be seen with the naked eye.

The language of the **logical-mathematical intelligence** is discernment of recurring patterns (including patterns that involve numbers, words, and geometric designs), problem-solving tactics, and strategies, and the encoding of concrete patterns in abstract symbols.

The language of **verbal-linguistic intelligence** is the spoken word (including formal and informal speaking), reading others' writing, writing (including poetry and persuasive writing), storytelling, linguistic humor (such as riddles, jokes, puns, limericks, and other twists of the language).

When you are concerned to awaken, stimulate, or activate these various ways of knowing in the brain-mind-body system, you must fully immerse yourself in the media of the various realms.

The single most important aspect of designing multiple intelligence assessments is to understand the unique cognitive processing mode of each intelligence. Our primary concern should be to create effective, intelligence-fair assessments, that is, *assessment tasks that honor the intellectual domain and the unique way of knowing for each intelligence.* The form and structure of the assessment must be true to the intelligence. For example, when using visual-spatial intelligence, you ask students to represent understanding using the media and cognitive processes appropriate to that intelligence, namely colors, designs, pictures, textures, shapes, images, patterns, and so on. Thus the form and structure of the assessment could involve such things as painting a mural, fabricating a diorama, sculpting something in clay, or creating a montage. Students must prove their understanding in and through the various forms they or you have chosen for the assessment.

When working with the intelligences in instruction, remember that, from a neurological point of view, *it is impossible to create a single-intelligence assessment task.* The human brain simply is not wired that way. By hook or by crook, all the intelligences will manage to weasel their way into the task because in normal people all the intelligences work together in a fairly well-orchestrated manner in almost any task we perform. I do *not* mean to suggest that no verbal dialogue should occur with students about what they have created or what they have performed. Students must be given a chance to explain, elaborate on, justify, and defend their work (including their written work!). However, you *can* design an assessment whose primary focus is one intelligence and that requires students to use the language and knowing modality of that intelligence to demonstrate their understanding of the concepts you are assessing.

In *Multiple Intelligence Approaches to Assessment* (1994), I present a menu of assessment ideas or instruments for structuring assessment tasks for the various intelligences. This menu (page 37) is intended to assist in the creation of multimodal or multiperceptual tests. The menu is not meant to be an exhaustive list of all possible assessment instruments, but rather a starting place for thinking about a much expanded approach to assessment, an approach to what I now call "multiple

Multiple Intelligence Assessment Menu

Verbal-Linguistic Intelligence
(Language Arts–Based Assessment Instruments)

- written essays
- vocabulary quizzes
- recall of verbal information
- audiocassette recordings
- poetry writing
- linguistic humor
- formal speech
- cognitive debates
- listening and reporting
- learning logs and journals

Logical-Mathematical Intelligence
(Cognitive Patterns–Based Assessment Instruments)

- cognitive organizers
- higher-order reasoning
- pattern games
- outlining
- logic and rationality exercises
- mental menus and formulas
- deductive reasoning
- inductive reasoning
- calculation processes
- logical analysis and critique

Visual-Spatial Intelligence
(Imaginal-Based Assessment Instruments)

- murals and montages
- graphic representation and visual illustrating
- visualization and imagination
- reading, understanding, and creating maps
- flowcharts and graphs
- sculpting and building
- imaginary conversations
- mind mapping
- video recording and photography
- manipulative demonstrations

Bodily-Kinesthetic Intelligence
(Performance-Based Assessment Instruments)

- lab experiments
- dramatization
- original and classical dance
- charades and mimes
- impersonations
- human tableaux
- invention projects
- physical exercise routines and games
- skill demonstrations
- illustrations using body language and gestures

Musical-Rhythmic Intelligence
(Auditory-Based Assessment Instruments)

- creating concept songs and raps
- illustrating with sound
- discerning rhythmic patterns
- composing music
- linking music and rhythm with concepts
- orchestrating music
- creating percussion patterns
- recognizing tonal patterns and quality
- analyzing musical structure
- reproducing musical and rhythmic patterns

Interpersonal Intelligence
(Relational-Based Assessment Instruments)

- group "jigsaws"
- explaining to or teaching another
- "think-pair-share"
- "round robin"
- giving and receiving feedback
- interviews, question-naires, and people searches
- empathic processing
- random group quizzes
- assess your teammates
- test, coach, and retest

Intrapersonal Intelligence
(Psychological-Based Assessment Instruments)

- autobiographical reporting
- personal application scenarios
- metacognitive surveys and questionnaires
- higher-order questions and answers
- concentration tests
- feelings diaries and logs
- personal projection
- self-identification reporting
- personal history correlation
- personal priorities and goals

Naturalist Intelligence
(Environment-Based Assessment Instruments)

- hands-on labs/demonstrations
- species/natural pattern classification
- nature encounters/field trips
- environmental feedback
- nature observations
- care for plants and animals
- sensory stimulation exercises
- conservation practices
- archetypal pattern recognition
- natural world simulations

representations of understanding." Part 2 outlines a set of performance rubrics for each instrument on the menu as well as provides some benchmarks to help assess students' understanding of the content being assessed in and through the various instruments. If you need specific examples of ways to apply any of the assessment instruments to traditional academic areas, see chapter 5 in *Multiple Intelligence Approaches to Assessment,* (Lazear 1994).

Performance Assessment: The Nature of the Beast

One final word about the nature of working with these kinds of assessments, what many today are calling "performance assessments." Howard Gardner (1993) calls these kinds of assessment "performances of understanding": "It is clear that understandings can only be apprehended and appreciated if they are performed by the student. We cannot know whether a student understands a principle . . . unless he can issue a relevant performance" (190).

Following are some general guidelines that I believe can help us as we move further and deeper into multiple intelligence approaches to assessment. As you consider these, bear in mind that throughout this book I operate out of three major presuppositions. (1) Assessment and instruction are two sides of a single coin. (2) The purpose of assessment is to enhance and deepen students' understanding of themselves, the curriculum, and the world in which they live. (3) If we are to realize the first two presuppositions, students must be assessed multimodally, or as Gardner says, they must be required to represent their understanding in various ways.

Performance Assessment Guidelines

1. *Students must know about the intelligences* and how to work within the unique language system and operating modality of each intelligence. It is very important to teach students about the eight intelligences. They must have opportunities to learn how to use each intelligence to represent what they know, understand, and have learned.

2. *Instruction must match the assessment.* In other words, if you are going to assess students using the multiple intelligences, it is crucial that you also teach using all the intelligences. Doing so will help students get some ideas of ways they can demonstrate their knowledge on the assessment. These kinds of assessments should be one with instruction. In fact, they are the flip side, so to speak, of instruction. We as teachers have no better instructional strategy in our kit bags than truly great, challenging, intelligence-fair assessments. Students participate in them and their learning is deepened.

3. The *rubrics or criteria for success on the assessment tasks must be clear,* in principle achievable by all, and public, that is, no secrets or surprises; everyone knows up front exactly what is expected and what is required.

4. The *cognitive process of the intelligences is more important than so-called artistic ability or talent.* Your primary interest is their demonstration or performance of their understanding. For example, whether or not a mural they produce would be considered "good art" is not the point. The question is "Have they demonstrated their understanding in and through whatever they have produced?" If talent development happens as a byproduct, great, but it is not the main goal.

5. *Scoring should focus on feedback about performance* with an eye toward helping students improve and move to a higher level of performance. In so doing you will move students to higher-order thinking and deeper understanding that goes beyond the popular and well-known "memorize-and-spit-back" approach. When considering any of the popular cognitive taxonomies in contemporary educational research, the so-called higher-order realms are synonymous with greater understanding, synthesis, integration, application, and generalization. Also, *avoid scoring practices that promote competition.* Score to promote self-competition and motivation to improve.

6. *Student participation in defining rubrics should be elicited.* You're after students investing in demonstrating their learning through the assessment. If you get questions such as, "What grade did you give me?" or "What grade did I get?" (as if it were a lottery), something's wrong.

7. *Assessment is a joint venture, something we do with students, not to them.* Our goal is to help students be their best, somewhat like the camaraderie between the drama teacher and students preparing for a play, or the coach preparing students for the big game.

8. *Authentic assessment is not (and never can be) a "lean, mean, efficient machine"*; however, if our goal is the thorough examination of students, an in-depth assessment of their learning, and preparing them for effective living in the twenty-first century (rather than simply getting a good score on an efficient, standardized test), then there is really no other choice! Can you imagine an executive at GM worried that it's going to take too much time to help workers produce a better product?

9. *Design rubrics that encourage students to perform at ever higher, more complex levels.* Generally you are encouraging them to perform at the higher-order or integral levels of the cognitive taxonomy for a given intelligence (see *Eight Ways of Knowing*). The more you can get them performing at these complex cognitive levels the greater will be their understanding and learning. Teach and practice ways to perform at the different rubric levels. Not all rubrics will apply to all subject areas, but, as in any performance, *the practice is the learning*.

The following chapters have several practical models for MI rubrics. What I present are not the only models possible. There are many right approaches to creating rubrics for multiple intelligence assessments. The most important thing about my models is they illustrate the principles and guidelines I mention above; principles and guidelines for creating rubrics that are authentic, intelligence fair, and brain compatible.

— Part 2 —

The Rubrics

An Introduction to MI Rubrics

Promoting Higher-Order Thinking and Understanding through Assessment

I n the next three chapters I present sets of rubrics for each instrument on the assessment menu. I call these "toward . . . rubrics" because I do not suggest that the rubrics I propose are the only "right" approach to creating fair rubrics. However, I hope to make a strong case for the fact that we can evaluate students' performances *and* their academic progress in many more effective ways than by focusing exclusively on verbal-linguistic or logical-mathematical assessments. What is more, if we are to thoroughly assess students we *must* move beyond the traditional paper-and-pencil assessments that we all know and love.

This attempt is my first to create rubrics for the various intelligences. Again, my passionate concern is that they be fair, which is to say they be brain compatible, standards based, and intelligence fair, so that they maximize and enhance students' learning through the assessment. Another concern is that they provide us with a truly accurate picture of where students are in their educational journey. I ask you to take the suggested rubrics and adapt them to your situation and amend areas you do not believe to be on target.

I have grouped the rubrics under the categories Howard Gardner used in his initial formulation of MI theory: the object-based intelligences, the object-free intelligences, and the personal intelligences. In the introduction to each chapter I explain each category. Each intelligence has a set of rubrics to assess the use of the instrument on the MI Assessment Menu and a set of generic content rubrics to assess understanding of content.

Toward Intelligence Performance Rubrics

I have created basic, complex, and higher-order rubrics for each intelligence. I used these same categories in *Eight Ways of Knowing* (1999a) to discuss the development pathway an intelligence takes. Here, as in *Multiple Intelligence Approaches to Assessment* (1994), I suggest that these same categories can be used as a taxonomy of performance, so to speak, to help us evaluate a student's use of a particular intelligence to perform a specific assessment task using the various instruments from the multiple intelligence assessment menu (111).

Basic Level

These rubrics generally outline a fairly simple, straightforward, linear performance. The performance involves a somewhat superficial or obvious use of the intelligence and utilizes the assessment instrument in an expected, safe manner (for example, simple word substitutions in an existing song or reproduction of a drawing very similar to one used for a model).

Complex Level

These rubrics reflect a performance that is multidimensional. The performance incorporates a variety of aspects of the intelligence and demonstrates an interesting, unusual use of the specific assessment instrument (for example, a simple flow chart or graph might incorporate the use of images, color, perspective, depth, and dimension; a role play might use simple props, costumes, sound effects, and clever characterization).

Higher-Order Level

These rubrics delineate a performance that shows a degree of mastery in the intelligence (the model essay, the classical mime, a quintessential mural) and a highly creative, unexpected use of the assessment instrument to convey application, transfer, synthesis, and integration of the learning (for example, using a Strauss waltz to illustrate frame-shifts in the genetic code or creating a diorama that incorporates ethnicity and cultural ancestry to show "why I'm an American, Canadian, Australian today").

As I mentioned in chapter 3, the main focus of these rubrics is to encourage students to perform at as high a level as possible, that is, at complex and involved cognitive levels within each intelligence. The rubrics are designed to help teachers and students recognize and assess understanding of the curriculum using the respective intelligences. They also provide feedback on areas of strength and areas that need growth. In your daily lessons, help students perform at the various levels so they have concrete examples of what those levels look like, as well as some practical experience. When you can get them performing at more complex cognitive levels, their excitement and involvement in the entire assessment process becomes real. They have a sense of ownership and pride in what they produce. And, what is more, their understanding and learning will be greatly amplified!

Toward Content Understanding Rubrics

My main concern for the content rubrics is to provide something that can be used and adapted for any specific subject area; therefore, for each instrument from the menu I have listed two sets of more or less generic questions. Please adjust them as necessary to fit your material, concepts, content, and so on.

Questions to Ask Myself

These questions are meant to help you become a "metacognitive detective," that is, an assessor who is passionately concerned to question his or her own assumptions and understanding enough to guarantee that students are given every conceivable opportunity to prove their understanding. The goal here is, of course, to ensure that students have been thoroughly examined. The second goal is to help you give conscious voice to questions about students' performance that you are probably already asking unconsciously.

Questions to Ask Students

These interactions are meant to be conversation starters that help you enter lively dialogues with your students. The assumption behind them is that this kind of dialogue with students often gives insight into their true understanding! The questions and statements are designed to help students get involved in the assessment process itself—they are asked to defend, justify, explain, and elaborate on their work. In this kind of active dialogue the assessment, teaching, and learning process truly become an integrated whole.

The questions and statements assume an active interchange between student and teacher that provide the student with the opportunity to defend the work. They also ensure that the teacher's thinking is in sync with the student's, and that the teacher understands the frame of mind from which the particular product was produced. Some of the questions and statements may have to be spiraled up or down to be appropriate for your students.

This approach to evaluating students' understanding is not only fair (we are asking students to explain things we may have missed and to defend their work), but it also helps us overcome our first, subjective, gut-level response to a performance or to compensate for a blind spot. The approach requires a careful and thoughtful analysis of students' work. We look at what they have produced and ask, "How and where, in and through what elements have they revealed their understanding of the required material?" The questions and statements also give students an opportunity to become co-partners in the assessment process, thus becoming responsible for their own assessment.

Intelligence Assessment Examples

The final sections of the three following chapters contain examples of various assessments that I have gathered from educational settings in the United States, Canada, and Australia. In most cases you will find the rubrics and the assessment of the final products.

These examples are works in progress, not finished, ideal assessment models. In fact, given the dynamic nature of human learning and development, I would be suspicious of the "perfect, finished assessment." You may also view these examples as MI assessment experiments that move beyond the linguistic-mathematical fallacy. None of the teachers who contributed examples claimed that the examples are right or perfect. But how else will we learn how to do MI assessments if we don't try, then learn from our experiments? I am profoundly grateful that these teachers were willing to share their voyages into mostly uncharted waters.

The examples are not necessarily a one-on-one demonstration of the rubrics I present; however, all of them illustrate the fact that *we can indeed move beyond current problematical assessment practices while maintaining solid, in-depth assessment of students' learning.* Sometimes what you will find in these examples are special projects or reports. Other examples show homework assignments. Some show formal tests that gave students options to use one or more intelligences. I hope these examples will give us courage to move our assessment practices in some very new directions as well as demonstrate how to maintain high standards.

I wish to extend very special thanks to the following teachers and their respective schools and districts who helped me compile these examples.

▶ Gloria Brudek
Sixth grade, Worth Junior High School, Worth, Illinois

Multiple intelligence theory embodies Gloria's beliefs in a dynamic learning environment. Nurturing students' various intelligences did not change what she taught; it changed how she taught. She believes MI enables all students to realize their full potential and contribute to the world in their own ways.

▶ Dale Burkholder
Brush High School, U.S. history, Memorial Junior High, South Euclid, Ohio

Always seeking alternative instructional strategies and techniques, Dale has participated in numerous professional development seminars throughout his career, including "Increasing Student Achievement in Your History Class," "Restoring the Narrative to American History," and "Strengthening Social Studies Instruction." Dale has incorporated multiple intelligence projects in his classroom as a means to individualize instruction and provide an alternative form of assessing student learning. He believes that, in today's diverse classroom environment, MI projects allow students to produce products in learning modes in which they may excel, and thus experience a degree of success that they may not have had with traditional assessment techniques.

▶ **Diane Callewaert**
General teacher, Colvin Elementary School, Wichita, Kansas

Diane first became interested in multiple intelligences while teaching students with learning disabilities, who require various strategies to learn. MI provided diversity and structure to Diane's lessons and planning. After she implemented an MI program, her students demonstrated enhanced learning in less time than before. She has been amazed at the progress her students have made due to MI strategies. She notes that "MI is the connection that allows my students' diverse needs to be linked with strategies that help them learn."

▶ **Jennifer Colasanti**
4th-grade teacher, Perrine Elementary School, Miami, Florida

Jennifer was a member of the initial multiple intelligence team in 1994 when Perrine Elementary began the action plan for a different way of teaching. She designed and formatted the multiple intelligence lesson plan form that Perrine teachers use.

▶ **Mauricette Hamilton**
Curriculum Advisor, Diocese of Ballarat, Mildura, Australia

Mauri has taught dance at St. Joseph's College in Mildura for twelve years. She has developed the years 7 through 10 course, which led to the Victoria Certificate of Education in study designs and dance and dance styles. She has also worked extensively in the area of dance in liturgy. Mauri combines ballet, jazz, modern and national dance with curriculum and standards. In the last three years, Mauri has worked in professional development to help teachers feel more confident in their ability to conduct dance and drama programs and motivate students with MI.

▶ **Jean L. Hopkins**
High school teacher, Spanish and English,
H.L. Richards High School, Oak Lawn, Illinois

Jean first became aware of multiple intelligences when her district decided to train a cadre of teachers. Since then she has been like a kid in a candy shop, delighting in using what she has learned because it involves her students in the process of their own learning and encourages them to continue that learning.

▶ **Michelle Jansky**
7th grade teacher, Memorial Junior High, South Euclid, Ohio

Michelle's curriculum revolves around four main topics: science and technology, matter, microbiology, and geology. Multiple intelligence theory sparked her interest when she attended Diane McFiggen and LouAnn Coffman's workshop in October 1996. She feels that students should be active participants in the learning process as they witness the applications of science to their personal lives. She believes that, although it may require more time to incorporate multiple intelligences into activities and assessments, the outcome of observing students "jump with excitement" because they have grasped a concept while having fun makes it all worth the effort.

Ann Krone
Educator, art, music, and gifted

Ann's first in-depth contact with multiple intelligences was at an ASCD conference in San Francisco. What she learned convinced her that many students who feel they are failures can change their minds about their abilities if they are taught in ways they learn best. As she studied MI, she implemented what she learned in her college art classes and saw the increased joy in learning her students experienced.

Sharon S. Neifer
Special education teacher, Bellevue High School, Bellevue, Ohio

As a special education teacher, Sharon finds multiple intelligences an exciting addition to education. She believes it allows all students to travel various avenues of intelligence to enhance their education instead of limiting them to the traditional methods. MI makes learning fun, which can be stressful for teachers but invigorating for students. MI levels the playing field so learning can take place through students' strengths instead of weaknesses.

Mary R. Porter
Adult and high school educator, job readiness and business, Bellevue High School, Bellevue, Ohio

Multiple intelligence theory has opened new doors for Mary. It provides an effective way to assess students' performance as it incorporates nontraditional classroom presentations. It allows students to learn in various ways, thus expanding and implementing their creativity. With MI, students are encouraged to explore their own potential. She finds that MI makes learning fun and finds it refreshing to explore new approaches in teaching and assessing.

Karen Rafacz
Facilitator of Title I freshman interdisciplinary program, Eisenhower High School, Oak Lawn, Illinois

Karen works with a team of teachers in English, math, science, and social studies who work with 120 at risk, underachieving ninth grade students. She became interested in multiple intelligences while searching for strategies to use with at-risk students to motivate them, "tune them back in" to school, and possibly reduce and prevent dropping out.

▶ **Todd Seman**
8th grade teacher, science, Memorial Junior High, South Euclid, Ohio

Todd believes that holding students accountable in today's society has become an increasing challenge that all teachers must meet. Authentic assessment plays an important role throughout Todd's grading system, which has allowed him to grasp students' attention quickly and apply difficult science concepts to real-life situations.

▶ **Becky Supercinski**
Gifted and talented teacher, Hudson PEP Elementary School, Longview, Texas

Becky writes her own curriculum and has presented at various gifted and talented workshops. In November 1995, she presented information from her unit on the brain and learning styles, "It's All in Your Mind," at the Texas Association for Gifted and Talented state conference in Austin, Texas. After reading several books on multiple intelligences and attending a workshop on MI assessment, she became interested in using the theory in her classroom. She now incorporates many of the MI principles in her teaching. She hosts an annual open house for parents in which students display products that reflect utilization of multiple intelligences.

4

Object-Related Intelligences
*Visual-Spatial, Logical-Mathematical,
Bodily-Kinesthetic, and Naturalist*_____

Performance Rubrics

In Howard Gardner's original research (1983), he suggested grouping visual-spatial, logical-mathematical, and bodily-kinesthetic intelligences under the category "object-related." In this work, I have included the naturalist intelligence in this group. Gardner notes that "the 'object-related' forms of intelligence . . . are subject to one kind of control: that actually exerted by the structure and the functions of the particular objects with which individuals come into contact. Were our physical universe structured differently, these intelligences would presumably assume different forms."

The object-related intelligences are based on the concrete shapes, patterns, colors, images, designs, and objects in the external world with which we come into contact and interact on a daily basis. These include not only the innumerable objects, shapes, patterns, colors, and so on that we encounter in the natural world, but also those that are created by humans—buildings, machines, art, inventions, and so on. It is the existence of these objects that trigger the related intelligences. In other words, with-out these objects to interact with, these intelligences would have nothing to do!

When using these intelligences, we consider how each expresses its special knowing as well as the actual stuff with which we must work. Rubrics must be firmly rooted in the following specific object bases for each of these four intelligences to fairly assess the object-related forms of intelligence.

Visual-Spatial

The visual aspect deals with everything we see: all conceivable shapes, specific patterns and designs (both regular and irregular), concrete and abstract images, and the entire spectrum of color and texture. What is more, all these objects exist not only in the real, concrete, external world (which we observe with our physical eyes), but also in the deep recesses of our imagination where we see with our mind's eye. These objects become apparent in our capacities to visualize and dream about the possible, to enter worlds of fantasy, to go on imaginary journeys to imaginary places, and to create or invent things that have never been before.

The spatial aspect deals with the relationships and placement of objects in the space and time continuum. Where one object is in relation to another is at the heart of the spatial aspect of this way of knowing. Knowing where you are in relation to objects that inhabit the space in which you live and being able to move successfully from one place to another are also part of this intelligence.

Bodily-Kinesthetic

The bodily aspect deals with elements that comprise our physical bodies, namely, arms, legs, head, torso, hips, shoulders, as well as internal organs such as the heart, brain, kidneys, blood, and bioneurological connectivity, down to the tiniest cells and their miraculous composition.

The kinesthetic aspect deals with the full range of movement that is possible in and through the body elements. This range includes not only those things that humans have achieved with the body, such as choreography that astounds us, mind-boggling physical feats in professional athletics, or theatrical performances that transport us beyond the mundaneness of daily living. It also includes the sometimes unrealized potentials of our innate kinetic abilities—the infant's potential to walk, the ability to develop and train gross and fine motor skills at almost any stage of our development, and the subtleties of what we can express through facial expressions, posture, and other so-called body language. I must also mention the latent potentialities of what contemporary researchers call the "kinesthetic body" or the "imaginal body." This is the body of muscular imagination through which we possess the ability, via active mental performance, to improve, strengthen, and refine the movements and functioning of the physical body.

Logical-Mathematical

The logical aspect deals with concrete, observable patterns that make rational sense; the object in these cases is the patterns themselves, which could include word patterns, visual patterns, even auditory and thought patterns. In principle, sounds and thoughts can be "object-tified" (that is, turned into concrete objects via concrete symbolization), thus making them observable to some degree.

The mathematical aspect deals with a very complex cognitive process that begins with what Jean Piaget called "concrete operational" thinking, that is, the process of hunting for and recognizing concrete patterns in the external environment. It then moves into the more involved process of understanding relationships among concrete patterns (for example, the processes of addition, subtraction, multiplication, and division). These cognitive processes increase in abstraction, ultimately becoming pure sumbols, namely, numbers. Thus, the objects of mathematics (especially higher-level math) are only there symbolically; for example, we can cognitively process a mathematical problem involving five women, thirteen artichoke hearts, and seven Macintosh computers without ever having to actually see them because the pure symbols "five," thirteen," and "seven" point beyond themselves to the physical, "concrete operational" realities.

Naturalist

The naturalist intelligence deals with many objects mentioned in the three previous descriptions, with one significant and defining difference: *all the objects are of the natural world,* and thus, humans had nothing to do either with their creation nor, in an ideal world, with their continued being. The dynamics and cognitive processes of the naturalist intelligence are primarily triggered by and related to patterns, images, designs, colors, textures, smells, tastes, sounds, and so on *that occur naturally.*

One of the more compelling aspects of research on the naturalist intelligence is finding that certain neural centers in the brain are devoted exclusively to the recognition, appreciation, and understanding of patterns, designs, and groupings *in the natural world* (as opposed to the human-created world). The capacities of the naturalist intelligence can be transferred to the human-created world, but those same capacities (the recognition, appreciation, and understanding of patterns, designs, and groupings in the human-created world) do not necessarily transfer to those same capacities and abilities in the natural world.

When we consider these object-based (or object-related) intelligences and the task of assessing students using them, it is important to remember that the assessments themselves must be couched in these object-related frameworks; that is, students must be required to work with objects of the various intelligences involved. The suggested instruments are designed to help us root ourselves within the unique cognitive reality of visual-spatial, bodily-kinesthetic, logical-mathematical, and the naturalist intelligences by requiring us to work with the unique media and within the language systems of the respective intelligences.

Assessing Visual-Spatial Intelligence

Visual-spatial assessments ask students to create visual displays and mental images through which their knowledge and learning can be evaluated. The primary mode of this form of assessment is the visual arts, including such things as painting, drawing, sculpting, imagining, and working with various hands-on manipulatives, as well as processes for seeing with the mind's eye using the active imagination.

Visual-spatial assessments require students to use active imagination, form mental images, recognize relationships of objects in space, imagine manipulations, and accurately perceive objects from various angles. Students must be able to demonstrate their learning and knowledge of the concepts being assessed using the language, tools, and media of visual perception (including both inner and outer seeing) and spatial relationships. They will use such things as images, designs, color, shapes, textures, pictures, visual symbols, and patterns in the assessment process.

Guidelines for Creating Visual-Spatial Content Rubrics

When you assess students using visual-spatial intelligence, you challenge them to prove their understanding of curricular concepts in visual-spatial ways. You must always be looking for this conceptual understanding in and through whatever they have produced. Remember, you are not assessing their so-called "artistic ability." Your main concern is with the cognitive process, the unique way of knowing represented by a specific visual-spatial product. The knowing that occurs in visual-spatial intelligence is embodied in shapes, colors, images, textures, designs, visual patterns and symbols, pictures, the active imagination, visualizations, daydreams, and logical and intuitive spatial relationships. The key is to learn to "read" and interpret these visual-spatial representations so you can discern students' actual understanding of the material.

Sample Rubrics for Visual-Spatial Intelligence

▶ ## Murals and Montages

Creating a collection of self-created or other-created images and pictures that show understanding

INTELLIGENCE PERFORMANCE

Basic-Level Rubric

- Use of single images or pictures that are obviously topic related

Complex-Level Rubric

- Use of variety of images that are creatively related to the topic

Higher-Order Rubric

- Use of many interrelated images that reveal complex understanding of and relation to the topic

CONTENT UNDERSTANDING

Questions to Ask Myself

- Do the various images created or incorporated have a clear relationship to the material?
- What images surprise me? Why am I surprised?
- What parts of the work require me to ask what the student is trying to express?

Questions to Ask Students

- "What are you expressing in this section of your work?"
- "Why did you include *x*?"
- "How does what you have drawn or represented in this part of your mural or montage relate to images in other parts?"

▶ Graphic Representation and Visual Illustration

Creating illustrations to show aspects, dynamics, or relationships within a topic

INTELLIGENCE PERFORMANCE

Basic-Level Rubric

- Use of simple, two-dimensional representations that mimic objects, shapes, designs, or patterns in the external environment

Complex-Level Rubric

- Use of visual depth, dimension, and perspective that more or less are literal representations of various scenes or objects

Higher-Order Rubric

- Use of impressionistic or expressionistic techniques or symbols that represent abstract concepts within a topic

CONTENT UNDERSTANDING

Questions to Ask Myself

- Where do I see clear representations of the content in the images, patterns, and colors?
- As I examine the illustration, where does my intuition tell me the student understands but I need to double-check?
- What totally baffles me? What do I find has no connections to the content at all?

Questions to Ask Students

- "I see *x* here, but could you please tell me about this part of your representation?"
- "I think I understand what you're communicating here, but could you tell me what this part means?"
- "How does what you have drawn in this part of your picture relate to other parts of the total work?"

Visualization and Imagination

Using mental imagery and the active imagination to create pictures in the mind about content, then describing those creations

INTELLIGENCE PERFORMANCE

Basic-Level Rubric

- Use of visualization exercises created by someone else and guided by someone else

Complex-Level Rubric

- Use of self-created or other-created exercises to guide oneself

Higher-Order Rubric

- Use of self-created and other-created visualizations to guide others

CONTENT UNDERSTANDING

Questions to Ask Myself

- As they discuss or process their experience of the exercise, do I sense they have seen their own images?
- At what points do I hear reports that they went beyond and embellished the images being suggested in the exercise?
- When did I observe students working together on the exercise to guide one another?

Questions to Ask Students

- "Tell me more about what you experienced in the exercise: What colors did you see? What did you smell? What did you hear? Taste?"
- "What happened when you had a chance to guide yourself? Was doing so easy or difficult? What did you do?"
- "What happened when you had a chance to guide others? Was doing so easy or difficult? What did you do?"

▶ Reading, Understanding, and Creating Maps

Creating legends to communicate spatial information or following directions on a map

INTELLIGENCE PERFORMANCE

Basic-Level Rubric

- Obvious, literal understanding almost totally derived from a legend

Complex-Level Rubric

- Interpretive understanding that demonstrates knowledge based on but going beyond a legend

Higher-Order Rubric

- Able to create own legend to communicate spatial relationships and directions

CONTENT UNDERSTANDING

Questions to Ask Myself

- As I look at the map, what do I see that leads me to believe the student understands more than what is shown?
- What do I not understand as I study the symbolic, spatial information the student has included?
- Where has the student gone beyond the normal legend and shown some unusual, creative aspects of the map?

Questions to Ask Students

- "I understand what these symbols show, but explain what these indicate."
- "Please take me on a tour of your whole map, explaining what I'll experience in each part (if you sense they understand more than what's shown)."
- "How would you help someone who has not been studying about legends understand yours (if they've gone beyond your expectations)?"

▶ Flow Charts and Graphs

Showing steps of various processes or operations, or presenting research findings from a project in a chart, flow chart, or graph

INTELLIGENCE PERFORMANCE

Basic-Level Rubric

- Demonstrates clear, linear (one-to-one) relationships among single independent items

Complex-Level Rubric

- Demonstrates multiple, linear relationships among several independent items

Higher-Order Rubric

- Demonstrates elaborate, linear and nonlinear relationships among all or most items

CONTENT UNDERSTANDING

Questions to Ask Myself

- Where do I see a clear connection between the information being assessed and its portrayal on the flow chart or graph?
- What on the flow chart or graph just doesn't make sense or is inaccurate?
- As I examine the flow chart or graph, what makes me think the student really understands but did not show it?

Questions to Ask Students

- "These parts of your flow chart or graph are absolutely on target, but these parts aren't. Talk to me about what is going on here."
- "I think you understand what you're trying to show in the flow chart or graph, but you've not shown it accurately here. How might you change it to make it accurate?"
- "If I hadn't been in this class, how would you explain to me what this flow chart or graph tells me?"

▶ Sculpting and Building

Constructing physical models that demonstrate stages of a process or inventing something based on learned concepts

INTELLIGENCE PERFORMANCE

Basic-Level Rubric

- Simple, obvious creations that duplicate real objects in the external world

Complex-Level Rubric

- Interpretive creations that show obvious relationships to real objects

Higher-Order Rubric

- Impressionistic or expressionistic creations that show abstract, symbolic, or metaphorical understanding

CONTENT UNDERSTANDING

Questions to Ask Myself

- Has the student created a model that accurately and clearly represents the key aspects of the concepts?
- Does the model incorporate the essential dynamics and relationships of the concepts?
- What parts of the construction seem out of place or have an unclear meaning?

Questions to Ask Students

- "What parts of your work please you the most and why?"
- "If you had to explain your creation to your parents so that they would understand what you've created, what would you say?"
- "I don't understand what this part of the sculpture or construction means."

▶ Imaginary Conversations

Pretending to have conversations with figures or characters from lessons or with various concepts or processes

INTELLIGENCE PERFORMANCE

Basic-Level Rubric

- Simple role-plays that involve real people having expected dialogues in obvious settings

Complex-Level Rubric

- Conversation with imagined people in a likewise imagined setting

Higher-Order Rubric

- Speaking from the perspective of an imagined person in imagined times and places

CONTENT UNDERSTANDING

Questions to Ask Myself

- What aspects of the required content are clearly incorporated in the imaginary conversation?
- What parts of the content did I sense as I listened between the lines?
- What was either not included or unclear?

Questions to Ask Students

- "When you said x, tell me more about what you were sensing and feeling as the character you were portraying."
- "Tell me how this character would respond to this situation."
- "In character, explain what this comment means."

▶ Mindscaping

Expressing understanding through visual maps that show colors, images, and relationships of something being studied

INTELLIGENCE PERFORMANCE

Basic-Level Rubric

- Mindscapes show clear and obvious, linear relationships between single ideas, concepts, or thoughts

Complex-Level Rubric

- Mindscapes demonstrate various complicated linear relationships and associations among several ideas, concepts, or thoughts

Higher-Order Rubric

- Mindscapes exhibit linear and nonlinear relationships and associations among clusters of ideas, concepts, or thoughts

CONTENT UNDERSTANDING

Questions to Ask Myself

- Are the fundamental concepts clearly represented in the mindscape?
- Has the student accurately shown the relationships or connections among the concepts?
- Where do I see something that just doesn't fit with the rest of the information presented?

Questions to Ask Students

- "How does this image on your mindscape relate to this image?"
- "I don't understand how this image fits in with the rest of what you've drawn on your mindscape. Can you help me understand?"
- "Which parts of your mindscape could you cluster?" OR "Can you explain why you clustered these items?"

▶ Video Recording and Photography

Reporting on field research for a project or taking photos that
illustrate understanding of certain concepts

INTELLIGENCE PERFORMANCE

Basic-Level Rubric

- Video footage or photographs record the obvious and expected facts
  (for example, a tree = tree)

Complex-Level Rubric

- Video footage or photographs show a thoughtful total composition
  (for example, tree = tree in surroundings)

Higher-Order Rubric

- Video footage or photographs present creative, unusual
  interpretation of the material being recorded (for example,
  tree = tree as symbol)

CONTENT UNDERSTANDING

Questions to Ask Myself

- Does the video footage or photograph clearly illustrate and relate to
  the content?
- Where have they presented the basic information but added some of
  their own creative aspects?
- What was really good in the presentation, but the relationship to the
  concepts is unclear?

Questions to Ask Students

- "I see very clearly your presentation of *x*, but talk to me about these
  other less obvious pictures you've included."
- "How do these images relate to the main topic or focus of your
  project?"
- "What made you think to include *x*?"

Manipulative Demonstrations

Working with various physical objects to show understanding of a concept or idea

INTELLIGENCE PERFORMANCE

Basic-Level Rubric

- Demonstration of simple, linear, one-to-one relationships, patterns, and connections

Complex-Level Rubric

- Demonstration of a variety of both linear and nonlinear relationships, patterns, and connections

Higher-Order Rubric

- Demonstration of a series of complex, nonobvious relationships, patterns, and connections

CONTENT UNDERSTANDING

Questions to Ask Myself

- As I watch the demonstration, where do I see clearly that they have understood the required concepts?
- What do I see in the demonstration that tells me they have a basic understanding but are still somewhat confused?
- Where do I feel I need to have them talk me through what they are doing and thinking as they work?

Questions to Ask Students

- "Do it again, but this time explain to me or a partner what you are doing." Ask questions, such as "Why are you doing that?"
- "I understand what you are doing until you get to x. Explain what you're doing then and why."
- "Explain how to apply your demonstration beyond school or in a new context."

Visual-Spatial Teacher Examples

World's Fair Display

The following example comes from Karen Rafacz. The activity is a very powerful example of ways to use visual-spatial intelligence to enhance, deepen, and expand students' understanding of material that is mostly prepackaged as verbal-linguistic. It shows ways MI can be used in conjunction with traditional research papers and special reports. The criteria that deal with appearance, knowledge, and oral presentation skills require some interpretation by the evaluator; that is, clear definitions of appearance, knowledge, and oral presentation for the various levels are not included. Students know from the beginning that they will be judged by outsiders and they know the exact criteria the judges will be using, very much like what occurs in Olympic competition. The project shows a nice balance between the performance and product and the understanding students display in and through their products.

The Activity

Teams create a display of a country to present orally at a World's Fair. They may use any materials to complete the project. They must work as a team to complete and include the following items:

1. **Geography**
   - Draw a map of the country with major cities, land forms, bodies of water, and border countries.
   - Research and write a report on the general location, population, capital, major cities, landforms, bodies of water, and famous landmarks.
   - Make a travel brochure.

2. **Culture**
   - Research and write a report on celebrations, religions, language, dress, food, art, and music.
   - Make a food, find and play a musical recording, or find a picture of a famous work of art.

3. **Flag**
   - Draw the flag.
   - Research and write a report on the meaning of the symbols and colors on the flag and the history of the flag.
   - Make a fabric flag.

4. History and Government

- Research and write a report on the early civilizations, invasions and wars, immigration and current form of government.
- Make a model of an artifact from history or find a picture of a famous leader.

5. Economy

- Research and write a report on the currency, natural resources, crops, industry, imports and exports, and tourism.
- Make a product map or draw the currency.

The Assessment

Teams are scored from 0 to 3 on the completeness of each element of their displays. They also receive scores from 0 to 3 on the appearance (neatness, color, good use of space, eye appealing), understanding of material, and oral presentation skills.

Food Group Cutouts

The next example is from Jennifer Colasanti; she developed it for a science and health unit. Note that the assessment happens in the midst of the instruction so the learning activities become the assessment. I am impressed with the beautiful simplicity (not simplistic) of the rubrics. The learning activity is fairly complex for early elementary, yet the assessment process and rubrics are easy, both to implement and for students to understand. The lesson is a fine illustration of a way to use the nontraditional intelligences to teach and assess traditional curricular concepts.

The Activity

The objective of this activity is to review what foods belong in which food group. Children bring in old magazines from which to cut pictures of foods. Children cut out pictures of foods from the various food groups. They come up one at a time and tape their food in the correct section of a photocopied food pyramid. In addition to the visual-spatial intelligence, the activity addresses the logical-mathematical and intrapersonal.

The Assessment

Students are assessed primarily on how well they choose foods from every food group to form a balanced meal. 1 point is given for every food group correctly represented for a possible 5 points.

Shape Pictures

The next example is also from Jennifer Colasanti. She developed it to reinforce shapes in her math unit. All comments about the previous activity, Food Group Cutouts, apply to this activity, as well.

The Activity

The objective of this activity is for students to correctly identify shapes and colors, and to teach listening skills. Students make pictures out of geometrical shapes (robots, houses, trees, boats, and so on) and photocopy them to pass out to students. Children then follow the teacher's directions, such as "Count the rectangles and circle the correct number; color them red. Then count the triangles and circle the correct number; color them blue." In addition to the visual-spatial intelligence, students must use verbal-linguistic and logical-mathematical intelligences.

The Assessment

The teacher designates points for correctly identifying the various shapes. You might give 3 points to students who identify all shapes, circle the correct numbers, and color them as directed. You might give 2 points to students who have circled the correct numbers but haven't colored as directed. Finally, you might give 1 point to students who did not count correctly but have colored some shapes appropriately.

Developing Classroom Rules

The next example is also from Jennifer Colasanti for use in a social studies unit. All comments about Food Group Cutouts apply to this activity, as well.

The Activity

The objective is to make children aware of the importance of rules and give them some say in the rules of the class. The class discusses rules and their benefits in general, then discusses classroom rules and how they help the class work effectively. They brainstorm and web four to six rules that would benefit their community. Students are placed in groups to design a sign that illustrates their assigned rule. In addition to the visual-spatial intelligence, verbal-linguistic, interpersonal, and intrapersonal intelligences are required.

The Assessment

The teacher, either alone or with students, develops four criteria for evaluating the signs. Signs are scored based on students' use of those criteria. Possible criteria include the following:

1. Rules must show at least one positive behavior.
2. Each rule must contain a consequence.
3. Everyone in your community must understand rules.
4. Illustrations must contain at least four colors.

Students who meet all four criteria will receive an A, three a B, two a C, and one a D.

Geography Puzzles

In the following example, Diane Callewaert's students work in cooperative groups to demonstrate understanding of the geographical location of five U.S. states using primarily visual-spatial intelligence and, to a lesser degree, musical-rhythmic. Following the description of the basic learning and assessment activity is a very thoughtful rubric that begins with the standard to be achieved, then proceeds through four performance levels. The most helpful element in each level is the evidence; Diane provides very practical and specific guidelines by which a teacher can tell at what levels students are performing and understanding. Another strength of this rubric is the clear set of guidelines it gives students so they can aim for a high-level performance and actively monitor their work and progress.

The Activity

Students are placed into cooperative groups of three or four. They are assigned the roles of leader, recorder, cheerleader, materials manager, and work cooperatively to draw and label Kansas and its bordering states. They cut the states apart and discuss the directional words that will help them reassemble their newly created puzzle. They develop an original song that will convey the way the puzzle pieces are to be reassembled. Students cooperate to present their song and puzzle to the class.

The Assessment

- Level 4: Students demonstrate their understanding of the location of Kansas and its bordering states by assembling puzzle pieces and singing their original song that tells them how. Evidence: Correctly labeled states are the correct shape and sized to scale so that all pieces fit together; song's tune is original and gives accurate information; directions in song correspond to precise actions in puzzle assembly.

- Level 3: Students demonstrate their understanding of the location of Kansas and its bordering states while singing a song and assembling puzzle pieces. Evidence: Correctly labeled states are the correct shape and four puzzle pieces fit together; song has a familiar tune and accurate information; song is presented; puzzle assembly is presented and explained.

- Level 2: Students demonstrate understanding that states have various sizes and locations, and tell location of each state in relation to Kansas by singing a song. Evidence: States have basic shapes, and two or three puzzle pieces fit together; song's tune is familiar and some information is accurate; song is partially presented and puzzle assembly is presented.

- Level 1: Students show no understanding of states and their positions. Evidence: States are not correct shapes and puzzle pieces do not fit together; song's tune is not easily discernible and information is inaccurate; method of assembling puzzle is not clear.

Bridges Project

This lesson and assessment teach and assess logical-mathematical content in visual-spatial and bodily-kinesthetic ways. The lesson and assessment come from Todd Seman. The entire focus is application of information. Simple recall is no use to students here! Although there is no rubric, the criteria by which students will be scored is in context; that is, projects are scored based on the very information students are supposed to be learning. This lesson is an excellent example of one main purpose of this book: assessment must be one with instruction and it must require students to demonstrate their understanding.

The Activity

After force and structure have been discussed in class for about one or two weeks, students form a company of two and give their companies names. Each pair is given a budget of $500,000 to build a bridge out of Popsicle sticks or toothpicks. They must include a blueprint drawn to scale and must be within the specifications under the assessment. After points are given, a percentage grade is determined. Material costs are as follows:

- 25 sticks and glue cost $385,000
- 10 sticks and glue cost $175,000
- 5 sticks and glue cost $95,000
- 1 stick and glue cost $55,000
- Consultant fee is $250/minute or $1,000/5 minutes
- Building permit costs $1,000
- Blueprints cost $12,000
- Fee for adjustments to blueprints during construction is $1,000/change
- Late fee is $1,500/day

The Assessment

1. Blueprints to scale

- Directions (2 views and a key in pencil) (15 points)
- Neatness (20 points)
- Accuracy (20 points)

2. Bridge specifications

- Length: 24 cm (10 points)
- Width: 6 cm (10 points)
- Mass: no more than 35 gms (10 points)
- Must include a deck and 2 sides; roof is optional (5 points)

3. Budget: $500,000

- Over budget (10 points)
- At budget (15 points)
- $1 to $9,999 under budget (17 points)
- $10,000 or more under budget (20 points)

4. Overall appearance (25 points)

Assessing Bodily-Kinesthetic Intelligence

Bodily-kinesthetic assessments ask students to express their learning and knowledge through practical demonstration or action. The primary mode of this assessment is physical movement, including physical exercise, physical games, and dramatic enactments. These assessments also include micromovements (what are often called "fine motor movements").

Bodily-kinesthetic assessments require students to show their understanding through various motor activities, including voluntary, involuntary, and preprogrammed body movements; through the connection of the mind and the body; through an expanded awareness of the body; through the improvement of body functioning; and through the development of mimetic abilities. Students must be able to "em-body" their learning and knowledge of the concepts being assessed using the language and tools of the body. They will use such things as dance, drama, gestures, role-play, expressive body language (facial expressions and postures), mime, and charades.

Guidelines for Creating Bodily-Kinesthetic Content Rubrics

When you assess students through bodily-kinesthetic intelligence, you challenge them to prove their understanding of certain curricular concepts in bodily-kinesthetic ways. You must always look for this conceptual understanding in and through whatever they have produced. Remember, you are not assessing their so-called athletic ability or their body coordination. Your main concern is with the cognitive process, the unique way of knowing represented by bodily-kinesthetic intelligence. The knowing that occurs in the bodily-kinesthetic intelligence is embodied in all forms and varieties of physical movement from the macro, or gross motor, to the micro, or fine motor. It thus involves such things as dance, drama, mime, role-play, physical gesture, physical games, and body language (facial expressions, postures, movement patterns, and so on). The key is to learn to "read" and interpret these bodily-kinesthetic representations for students' actual understanding of the material being assessed.

Sample Rubrics for Bodily-Kinesthetic Intelligence

▶ Lab Experiments

Successfully performing certain specified processes of an experiment

Basic-Level Rubric

- Experiment is performed successfully, step-by-step, with little reflection or thought about its meaning

Complex-Level Rubric

- Experiment is performed successfully and student expresses own thoughts, feelings, and questions about the experiment

Higher-Order Rubric

- Experiment leads student to connections, questions, thoughts, and reflections that go beyond the experiment

CONTENT UNDERSTANDING

Questions to Ask Myself

- Does the student show an understanding of the process versus merely going through the proper steps?
- Do conclusions, questions, or reflections on the experiment show understanding of the key concepts involved?
- Where does the student seem to be confused by the point of the experiment or what they are observing or discovering?

Questions to Ask Students

- "Talk me through the steps of the experiment and tell me why each is important to the whole."
- "What led to the conclusions you have drawn from the experiment? What more can you say about your reflections or questions?"
- "In your own words, explain what this experiment is all about. What if someone said 'So what?'"

▶ Dramatization

Enactments that show stages of various processes, events, or complex relationships of concepts

INTELLIGENCE PERFORMANCE

Basic-Level Rubric

- Literal enactment based exactly on the facts, events, processes, and concepts

Complex-Level Rubric

- Interpretive enactment with numbers of creative embellishments that show more than just the facts

Higher-Order Rubric

- Original enactment that shows contemporary social or personal implications, applications, and importance

CONTENT UNDERSTANDING

Questions to Ask Myself

- Where do I see the obvious connections between their drama (including props, costumes, and dialogue) and the content?
- Where do I see clever applications of the content in a new or different context?
- What parts of the dramatization seem to be off target or inappropriate given the content?

Questions to Ask Students

- "What was behind your thinking in the way you staged your drama (e.g., the costumes, props, setting, dialogue, and so on)?"
- "Can you help me understand how *x* fits in and why you included it?"
- "How would your dramatization change if *x* happened (throw in something unexpected from contemporary life)?"

▶ Original and Classical Dance

Choreographing an orchestrated flow of body movements that embody various concepts

INTELLIGENCE PERFORMANCE

Basic-Level Rubric

■ An elementary series of disconnected gestures and other movements involving minimal activity

Complex-Level Rubric

■ A complex series of well-orchestrated movements that actively engage and involve the whole body system

Higher-Order Rubric

■ Movement that is a true embodiment of the concepts (including appropriate gestures and facial expressions)

CONTENT UNDERSTANDING

Questions to Ask Myself

■ What connections do I see among the movements, steps, and flow of the dance and the concepts?

■ What movements seem out of place and not representative of the content?

■ Where do I sense a deep understanding of the required information? Where have they gone beyond my expectations?

Questions to Ask Students

■ "I understand what you are expressing in most of the dance, but please explain *x* to me."

■ "If you had to put narration with the dance, what would you say?"

■ "How would you change the dance if you were doing it for very young children? Very old people? Someone from another culture?"

▶ Charades and Mimes

Acting out or role-playing various concepts, facts, or ideas

INTELLIGENCE PERFORMANCE

Basic-Level Rubric

- Literal, to-be-expected, minimal acting out of the material

Complex-Level Rubric

- Clever and complex movements to communicate the material

Higher-Order Rubric

- Quintessential; you get so caught up in the student's performance you almost forget you're in school

CONTENT UNDERSTANDING

Questions to Ask Myself

- What are the unmistakable associations between the performance and the specific concepts, thoughts, or ideas?
- As I watch the charade or mime, where do I sense a deeper understanding than what is showing?
- What confuses me about the charade or mime because I see no connection to the content?

Questions to Ask Students

- "Do the charade or mime again, but this time explain what you're doing as you make the various movements."
- "If you were going to turn your charade or mime into a fifteen-minute TV show, what would you change (when you sense they understand more than shown)?"
- "What additional movements, actions, gestures, postures, or facial expressions could communicate the content?"

▶ # Impersonations

Becoming another person and acting, speaking, feeling, behaving as that person would in a given situation

INTELLIGENCE PERFORMANCE

Basic-Level Rubric

- Impersonation is very literal, employing only the given facts about the person being portrayed

Complex-Level Rubric

- Impersonation shows the addition of one's own creative thoughts and feelings

Higher-Order Rubric

- Portrayal is an incarnation of the other person, including contemporary significance

CONTENT UNDERSTANDING

Questions to Ask Myself

- Has the student accurately portrayed the basic information about the person?
- Do I sense a personal connection with, deep understanding of, or empathy with the person through the impersonation?
- Has the student shown a grasp of the person's importance or contributions to today?

Questions to Ask Students

- "Explain why you chose this person and your thinking behind how you portrayed them."
- "Why did you include x as part of your portrayal?"
- "If this person were to walk into x (situation from the news) how would he or she respond?"

▶ Human Tableaux

Using body sculpture to exhibit understanding; arranging a group of people into a living sculpture

INTELLIGENCE PERFORMANCE

Basic-Level Rubric

- Tableau is fairly obvious and shows a one-to-one linear understanding of basic facts (for example, one cause = one effect)

Complex-Level Rubric

- Tableau demonstrates a complex understanding that goes beyond the basic facts (for example, one cause = many, interrelated, unexpected effects)

Higher-Order Rubric

- Tableau is a true epitome of the concepts and processes and shows many levels of dynamic linear and nonlinear relationships

CONTENT UNDERSTANDING

Questions to Ask Myself

- Does the tableau include all of the pieces of the concept?
- Is the student able to explain the dynamic relationships among the various parts of the tableau as it relates to the content?
- What aspects of the tableau do not clearly show the relationship to the concepts?

Questions to Ask Students

- "If this human sculpture were on display at the art institute, what would you name it? How would you label its parts?"
- "If you had to write three sentences about your tableau to help someone who's not in our class understand, what would you say?"
- "I don't understand this part of your tableau. Please explain it to me."

▶ # Inventions

Creating various products to show understanding and application of learning

INTELLIGENCE PERFORMANCE

Basic-Level Rubric

- Nonoriginal idea developed in a linear, expected manner that incorporates basic facts

Complex-Level Rubric

- Original idea developed in multidimensional ways that goes beyond and is creative with the basic facts

Higher-Order Rubric

- Original idea developed in unusual, unexpected ways that show applications and implications of basic concepts

CONTENT UNDERSTANDING

Questions to Ask Myself

- Are all the basic facts, concepts, and so on accurately represented in some manner?
- Where does the project show an understanding that goes beyond "the facts, ma'am; nothing but the facts"?
- What do I see in the project that shows an understanding that the concepts presented in the project are applicable beyond the project itself?

Questions to Ask Students

- "I don't see x, y, or z in your project. Please tell me why."
- "Explain to me what new discoveries you made by doing this project? What did you find most interesting or exciting?"
- "If someone saw your project then asked you 'So what? Why is this important?' what would you say?"

▶ Physical Exercise Routines and Games

Creating movement exercises and games that utilize various concepts, facts, and ideas

INTELLIGENCE PERFORMANCE

Basic-Level Rubric

- Simple, could-be-anticipated use of the concepts, facts, and ideas

Complex-Level Rubric

- Creative, unexpected incorporation and application of the concepts, facts, and ideas

Higher-Order Rubric

- Creative use of concepts, facts, and ideas that make them an integral part of the games or exercise itself

CONTENT UNDERSTANDING

Questions to Ask Myself

- Do I see clear connections between the games or exercise and the concepts being assessed?
- What do I see that intrigues me, but I still need clarification?
- What leads me to wonder if the student has really understood the concepts?

Questions to Ask Students

- "Explain how this game or exercise routine relates to what we're studying and learning."
- "I find this part of your game or exercise very interesting. Explain your thinking in including it."
- "If you were to change the game or exercise to *x*, how would you change it?"

▶ Skill Demonstrations

Demonstrating understanding of a topic through proficient execution of related activities, skills, and abilities

INTELLIGENCE PERFORMANCE

Basic-Level Rubric

- Skill demonstration is accurate and is executed consciously, carefully, step-by-step

Complex-Level Rubric

- Skill demonstration is accurate with some measure of precision (shows confidence in skill)

Higher-Order Rubric

- Skill is an integrated part of one's being; precision performance ("second nature" execution)

CONTENT UNDERSTANDING

Questions to Ask Myself

- Am I seeing accurate execution of the related skills, activities, and abilities?
- Where am I seeing extraordinary performance of the skill and a deep understanding of its relationship to the topic?
- Where do I sense confusion by the skills, activities, and abilities and how they relate to the content?

Questions to Ask Students

- "Tell me how performing this skill helps you more fully understand and appreciate the concepts we've been studying."
- "Why is this skill, activity, or ability important? How could you communicate the importance to someone who's not studied it as much as you?"
- "How does knowing this skill affect you personally?"

▶ Illustration through Body Language and Gestures

Making appropriate physical signals and postures to illustrate concepts or ideas

INTELLIGENCE PERFORMANCE

Basic-Level Rubric

- Body language and gestures illustrate literal and obvious single elements (for example, sadness = making a sad face)

Complex-Level Rubric

- Complex, dynamically interrelated display of gestures, facial expressions, postures, and so on to illustrate multiple aspects of the material

Higher-Order Rubric

- Body illustrations show layers of complexity including the addition of one's own creative interpretation and experience

CONTENT UNDERSTANDING

Questions to Ask Myself

- Do I sense a genuine understanding of the relationship between the body language and what the student is trying to communicate?
- Where do the body language and gestures seem to be mismatched?
- What do I see that leads me to think there is deeper understanding than what the student is able to show?

Questions to Ask Students

- "Why did you decide on *x* to communicate *y*?"
- "Explain the thinking and feelings behind your body language and gestures."
- "I don't understand how *x* go with the concepts you are trying to communicate. Help me understand."

Bodily-Kinesthetic Teacher Examples

Rhyming Words

This example is from Jennifer Colasanti for use in a language arts unit. Note that the assessment, as do her earlier examples, happens in the midst of the instruction so the learning activities become the assessment. I am impressed with the beautiful simplicity (not simplistic) of the rubrics. The learning activity is fairly complex for early elementary. The assessment process is rather traditional in that students are given points for correct answers. The lesson is a fine illustration of a way to use the nontraditional intelligences to teach and assess traditional curricular concepts.

The Activity

The objective of this activity is to reinforce students' understanding of rhyming words. The class discusses what a rhyme is; the teacher gives examples of words that rhyme. Students stand where they can't see one another, such as in a circle facing out. The teacher says two pairs of words at a time, one that rhymes and one that doesn't. Students clap once for the pair that rhymes and stomp once for the pair that doesn't rhyme. As an alternative, teachers could come up with a list of activities that have words that rhyme ("Touch your nose and toes"; "Touch your hair and point to the air") and activities with no rhyming words ("Open your mouth and stomp your feet"). Students perform only the actions that have rhyming words. In addition to the bodily-kinesthetic intelligence, logical-mathematical and intrapersonal intelligences are used.

The Assessment

The teacher gives points for each correct action and converts scores to a percentage for the grade.

Addition and Substraction

This example is from Jennifer Colasanti for use in a math unit. The comments from the previous activity, Rhyming Words, apply here, as well.

The Activity

The objective of this activity is to reinforce addition and subtraction skills. Children clap answers to several called-out addition problems and stomp answers to several subtraction problems. The problems are then mixed, with students clapping answers to addition problems and stomping answers to subtraction problems. In addition to bodily-kinesthetic intelligence, logical-mathematical and intrapersonal intelligences are used.

The Assessment

The teacher assesses students during the activity by giving points for correct use of corresponding movement and documenting the information on a copy of the seating chart to make efficient use of time. Students are given points according to how many problems they solve correctly using the appropriate kinesthetic response.

Choreography of Roald Dahl's "Witches"

The following example comes from Mauri Hamilton. It is an excellent example of a way to integrate the fine arts with academics. The discussion that takes place throughout the project illustrates a way to use rubrics from the very beginning of a unit. Mauri includes assessment ideas, although she does not delineate various levels of mastery. The unit reflects a fine integration of or wedding between the assessment and instruction process. From the outset, students are preparing to perform for other people, so they are always looking to make the performance as good as possible, putting them in an assessment mode. The rubrics become no big deal to develop because they are part and parcel of preparing for the performance. You might even want students to help you develop rubrics according to Mauri's assessment ideas so they fully understand what is expected of them.

The Activity

Students and teacher read Roald Dahl's "Witches." Under the teacher's direction, students practice various movements and learn movement vocabulary to "I Just Can't Wait to Be King." Students and teacher brainstorm ideas about various body postures that would depict witches they have read about or seen in films or on television. Students then improvise, using the brainstormed suggestions to create postures that depict witches—ugly, scary—and a "nice" woman—smart, kind, happy, confident. They link both shapes with a run, jump, roll, and slide. The teacher directs them to use 8 or 16 counts to complete their movement and reminds them always of including high, medium, and low levels in their jumps and direction changes (forward, backward, sideways, up, down, diagonal) in their rolls and slides. Students also improvise the basketball game in the story.

Students choose a piece of music and one part of the story line from "Witches." They create a dance with at least two sections and a transition between. The two sections should contrast so students can use a wide scope of movement. For example, one movement would involve students who are "nice" and turn into witches in the second movement. Students don't have to follow the original story slavishly but can use it as a stimulus for creative choreography.

After completing the choreography, students work on the performance and present their dance at a school concert. They are responsible for simple costumes, props, scenery, and make-up.

The Assessment

While students are improvising and making their dance, constantly discuss the work. Students should be asked to state preferences for various sequences, always stating why the sequence appealed to them. They should also discuss the use of levels, directional changes, movement vocabulary, variations in rhythmic patterns, body actions, dynamics, unity of sequences, motifs, and gestures. The final composition should be unified and students should be able to identify a clear beginning, development, and conclusion. Students should also keep a journal that records their progress in all activities, including a description of the structure of the dance, the movement vocabulary, and sequences and diagrams of their movements. If you have access to a camcorder, you could also videotape the performances and discuss them as a class.

Ideas for assessment include how well students do the following:

Learn movement vocabulary

Sustain character

Vary levels, direction, dimension, unison, canon, and contrast

Invent movement

Use variety of dynamics

Perform movement skillfully

Observe and imitate movement of others

Respond rhythmically

Work with a group

Be expressive

Organize movement on a given theme

Teach movement sequences to others

Create a unified composition

Maintain focus and sequence

Devise appropriate costumes

Devise performance elements as required

Discuss their work using correct dance terminology

Keep a journal of their work

Music Mime

Following is another fine example from Mauri Hamilton that shows a way to integrate the fine arts with academics. It uses storytelling and story creating. Students make use of bodily-kinesthetic intelligence through the medium of mime. The musical-rhythmic and visual-spatial intelligences are also used as students add an appropriate musical background to their story and create props, costumes, and so on. The class discussion reflects ways the rubrics kick into gear during students' *preparation* for the performances.

The Activity

The class discusses the concept of a music mime, that is, a mimed story set to music. They view a silent movie or a mimed sequence. They discuss the era in which these were developed. They then mime a variety of situations that involve very simple actions, such as brushing their teeth. To be effective, the movements must be exaggerated. Individual students mime an action for the class as the class tries to guess what the action is. Possible subjects include a person or profession and television advertisements.

Students form groups and choose from a selection of one- to two-minute instrumental pieces that have a clearly established beat and that cover a range of tempos. They also choose a story line that matches the music. They create and rehearse to refine movement sequences to produce a mimed story. The story may be an original or a retelling. The action must fit the exact length of the music and interpret the musical piece in some way. Students will choose the space, props, costumes, and setting for their performance. The audience can be the class or an outside audience. Along the way, students record their creation process in work books. They may include written reports, journal entries, pictures, and videos. They also research the silent movie or video.

The Assessment

During the creation of the mime, students discuss the elements that make a mime successful. The dimension of movement is important, as are the performance space, their postures and movement patterns. Students also discuss reasons for their choices of music and their use of costumes and props to enhance the performance. After the performance, the class offers positive comments first, then constructive criticism. Ideas for assessment include the following:

> *Ability to use posture and movement to portray a character*
>
> *Ability to improvise*
>
> *Ability to select and refine*
>
> *Ability to work in a group*
>
> *Ability to move in time to the music*

Ability to use the performance space effectively

Ability to use costumes and props

Ability to remember sequences and maintain concentration

Ability to sustain character

Ability to participate in class discussion using correct dramatic terminology

Ability to maintain a work book that outlines the creation process

Ability to present an oral or written report that demonstrates an understanding of some aspect of the silent movie era

Assessing Logical-Mathematical Intelligence

Logical-mathematical assessments ask students to show what they have learned through logical, analytical, rational thought processes. The primary mode of this form of assessment is finding, recognizing, understanding, and utilizing patterns, including abstract number patterns, word patterns, and more concrete, object-based visual and tactile patterns.

Logical-mathematical assessments require students to use abstract pattern recognition, inductive and deductive reasoning, discerning logical relationships and connections, performance of varieties of complex calculations, and scientific reasoning. Students must be able to demonstrate their learning, knowledge, and understanding by solving various kinds of subject- or curriculum-related problems and by explaining the patterns and rationales of the specific content being assessed.

Guidelines for Creating Logical-Mathematical Content Rubrics

When you assess students through the logical-mathematical intelligence, you challenge them to prove their understanding of certain curricular concepts in logical and mathematical ways. You must always look for this conceptual understanding in and through whatever they have produced. Remember, you are not assessing if they are a math whiz, so to speak, or if their logic could outwit an attorney. The knowing that occurs in the logical-mathematical intelligence is embodied in the search for, discovery of, and desire to understand patterns and in the challenge of solving a problem or hunting for ways to deal with a challenge.

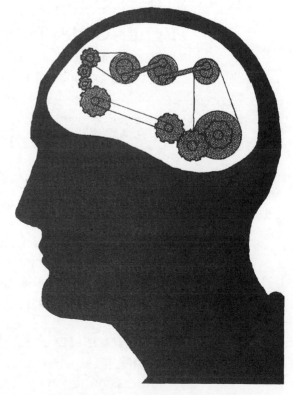

It involves such things as understanding patterns, use of numbers to reflect patterns, understanding various logical thinking strategies and patterns and when to use them, the calculation of known and unknown quantities, and the employment of the scientific method of investigation. The key is to learn to read and interpret these logical-mathematical representations for students' actual understanding.

Sample Rubrics for Logical-Mathematical Intelligence

▶ Cognitive Organizers

Using various thinking pattern maps such as webs, Venn diagrams, and classification matrices to demonstrate understanding

INTELLIGENCE PERFORMANCE

Basic-Level Rubric

- Uses one or two organizers to show factual, obvious, to-be-expected information

Complex-Level Rubric

- Uses a variety of organizers to show understanding

Higher-Order Rubric

- Uses a variety of organizers in creative ways to show applications and implications of the material

CONTENT UNDERSTANDING

Questions to Ask Myself

- Where do I see clever or unusual use of various cognitive organizers?
- Where did the student use the organizers correctly but the information is inaccurate?
- Where do I sense that the student truly understands the information but did not use the organizer correctly?

Questions to Ask Students

- "Why did you decide to use the various organizers you used? What others could you have used?"
- "Explain what this organizer is showing about the information."
- "The information is not quite right. Can you do the same thing with this accurate information?"

▶ Higher-Order Reasoning

Moving from factual recall through process to understanding, to synthesis and integration when thinking about or learning something

INTELLIGENCE PERFORMANCE

Basic-Level Rubric

- Accurately recalls the basic facts, figures, concepts, and main ideas of the material

Complex-Level Rubric

- Shows an understanding of the relationships, dynamics, process, and connections among the bits and pieces of the information

Higher-Order Rubric

- Demonstrates a coherent understanding of the material by showing its applications and implications beyond the school setting

CONTENT UNDERSTANDING

Questions to Ask Myself

- Where am I confused by connections that don't seem to relate to the information?
- What has the student seen and understood that is beyond my expectations?
- Where does the student seem to be confused by the basic facts?

Questions to Ask Students

- "Help me understand how you got from *x* to *y*."
- "What are the main points you started with in your thinking? Are you sure they are accurate and that you understand?"
- "Tell me how and why this information is important beyond something you must learn in school."

Pattern Games

Demonstrating understanding of a subject through recognition or reproduction of its patterns

INTELLIGENCE PERFORMANCE

Basic-Level Rubric

- Recognizes the most obvious, simple patterns, often those that have been previously pointed out by another person

Complex-Level Rubric

- Identifies obvious patterns but also discerns the more subtle, not-so-obvious patterns

Higher-Order Rubric

- Creates new patterns using the existing patterns; demonstrates an integral understanding of the inherent patterns

CONTENT UNDERSTANDING

Questions to Ask Myself

- Where has the student created a clever game but without a clear, understandable pattern?
- What patterns are obvious and what patterns has the student neglected to include?
- Does the student understand the patterns and their implications?

Questions to Ask Students

- "Tell me about your game and the patterns you have included."
- "I see the patterns. How would you explain them to someone who is not in our class?"
- "Let's take the game further. Can you find this pattern? How can you include this pattern?"

▶ Outlining

Showing one's grasp of a subject by listing main points, subpoint, subpoints of the subpoints, and so on

INTELLIGENCE PERFORMANCE

Basic-Level Rubric

- Outline contains main points and subpoints that show a one-on-one, expected, linear understanding

Complex-Level Rubric

- Outline contains main points, subpoints, and sub-subpoints that show a number of clever logical connections

Higher-Order Rubric

- Outline is quintessential, that is, perfectly logical, with all points clearly related to the main points

CONTENT UNDERSTANDING

Questions to Ask Myself

- Does the outline logically connect all the way down to the sub-subpoints?
- Where do I sense that the student understands the material but the outline doesn't convey the understanding?
- What confuses me?

Questions to Ask Students

- "Explain how this point relates to what's above and below it" (when they understand but the outline doesn't show it).
- "Would you please talk me through your outline, explaining each new level?"
- "If you had to take the outline down one more level, how would you do it?"

Logic and Rationality Exercises

Exhibiting understanding and knowledge through various syllogisms or "if . . . then" statements

INTELLIGENCE PERFORMANCE

Basic-Level Rubric

- Straight-line, linear reasoning based wholly on the given or beginning information

Complex-Level Rubric

- Creative (but logical) leaps in thinking about the material being assessed by going beyond the beginning information

Higher-Order Rubric

- Applications and implications of the material go beyond the classroom

CONTENT UNDERSTANDING

Questions to Ask Myself

- Where am I "not inside" the thought processes; that is, it seems illogical?
- Has the student gone beyond the basic facts to explore some of their meanings and connections to other things?
- Is the student seeing the logical implications in the content? Is it making sense?

Questions to Ask Students

- "I'm interested in some of your thoughts about how to use this information. Please tell me more."
- "What you say here doesn't make sense to me. Can you explain your thinking?"
- "What would you say if you had to explain this to someone much younger than you?"

Mental Menus and Formulae

Using acrostics, acronyms, and other kinds of formulae to prove one's knowledge

INTELLIGENCE PERFORMANCE

Basic-Level Rubric

- Simple menus or formulae that show a fairly linear connection to the material

Complex-Level Rubric

- Menus demonstrate many connections that go beyond a mere recording and recounting of the facts and figures

Higher-Order Rubric

- Ingenious and clever menus and formulae show deep understanding of the material

CONTENT UNDERSTANDING

Questions to Ask Myself

- As I examine the menus or formulae, do I feel that the student understands the deep meanings?
- What really seems out of sync in the menu or formulae? What do I need to ask them to explain?
- Where has the student displayed information via a menu or formula that is inaccurate?

Questions to Ask Students

- "I don't understand your thinking with this particular menu or formula. Please explain it further."
- "Tell me more about what the information on your menu means. How is it useful?"
- "What you have on your menu is not quite right. Can you make a new one with this information?"

Deductive Reasoning

Showing one's ability to sort or classify specific information into general categories

Basic-Level Rubric

- Information is grouped into preexisting, expected categories based on previously learned material

Complex-Level Rubric

- Information is grouped into surprising new categories with new and creative names

Higher-Order Rubric

- Information is grouped into general classifications that show a complex understanding by forcing a new gestalt of the information

Questions to Ask Myself

- What leads me to believe the student understands the large categories, but maybe not the details?
- What details do I feel the student understands without knowing how to fit them into the larger categories?
- Where has the student used the general categories in creative or unusual ways that I need to ask him about?

Questions to Ask Students

- "In your own words, tell me what the large categories mean and how you would tell if something fits in them."
- "I find your classification very interesting. Can you tell me how you arrived at it?"
- "What criteria did you use to help you decide to fit x detail into y category?"

▶ Inductive Reasoning

Showing one's ability to reach conclusions or create general categories based on specific details

INTELLIGENCE PERFORMANCE

Basic-Level Rubric

- Draws conclusions wholly based on and related to the facts and figures of the material; sees only one possible conclusion

Complex-Level Rubric

- Draws surprising conclusions but is able to justify conclusions based on the material

Higher-Order Rubric

- Interprets details to show a variety of plausible conclusions; sees implications of the material for own life

CONTENT UNDERSTANDING

Questions to Ask Myself

- Is the student drawing conclusions from the details that I can't understand?
- Is the student seeing all possible conclusions that might be made?
- Where has the student made surprising conclusions that I need to ask her to explain?

Questions to Ask Students

- "Please walk me through the process you used to get to this conclusion."
- "If you had to come up with two more possible conclusions based on these details, what would they be?"
- "What if x, y, and z details changed? How would this change or not change your conclusions?"

▶ # Calculations

Exhibiting understanding by employing various problem-solving strategies

INTELLIGENCE PERFORMANCE

Basic-Level Rubric

- Employs only those strategies that have been previously taught or used

Complex-Level Rubric

- Uses previously learned problem-solving strategies in new and creative ways

Higher-Order Rubric

- Invents new strategies based on but not controlled by previously learned strategies

CONTENT UNDERSTANDING

Questions to Ask Myself

- Has the student used the proper process for the problem or challenge at hand? Did the student use it correctly?
- Where did the student use the right process but arrive at an inaccurate conclusion?
- Where am I confused by the answers and how the student came up with them?

Questions to Ask Students

- "How did you decide which processes to use in solving this problem?"
- "Walk me back through your problem-solving process and show me how you got this answer."
- "You used the right process but didn't get the right answer. Please go through it again and catch your mistakes."

▶ Logical Analysis and Critique

Demonstrating knowledge of a subject by applying a discipline such as literary criticism or the scientific method

INTELLIGENCE PERFORMANCE

Basic-Level Rubric

- Surface, linear application of analytical techniques to the material; sticks to analyzing the basic facts and most obvious aspects

Complex-Level Rubric

- Unusual and provocative analytical methods that show thinking beyond the mere facts

Higher-Order Rubric

- Analysis of material using analytical and critique methods but also creating something new based on the material

CONTENT UNDERSTANDING

Questions to Ask Myself

- Where did the student lose me in the analysis; where do I need to ask for clarification?
- In the analysis or critique, where has the student made unexpected statements that I need to explore further?
- Did the student correctly employ the analytical tools and seem to understand what he was doing?

Questions to Ask Students

- "Please help me understand why and how your analysis led you to these conclusions."
- "Why did you choose to analyze this material in the way that you did? How did this affect your conclusions?"
- "What other analytical tools might you have used? How would you decide?"

Logical-Mathematical Teacher Examples

Scientific Method

This example is from Michelle Jansky. It deals with learning the scientific method. It demonstrates an ingenious way to help students develop one capacity of logical-mathematical intelligence. The first part of the lesson is an enjoyable, in-context experience of understanding and using the scientific method to make inferences and predictions relating to bubble gum. The second assumes the basic understanding of the first lesson and goes beyond to deepen, expand, and enhance students' understanding of each step of the scientific method. Both activities have real-life applications. The grade report, while not a rubric, clearly shows a way criteria can be used to value each distinct aspect of the logical-mathematical performance.

The Activity

Students first test four brands of bubble gum. They answer a series of questions based on their reading of an article. The questions ask them to define certain words related to bubble gum and state other facts that will be pertinent to their experiment. They make some predictions and inferences, including predicting which brand of gum will allow them to blow the biggest bubbles, and inferring why chewed gum has less mass than unchewed gum and why chewed gum loses its flavor. They then create an investigative question and a hypothesis, state a manipulated variable and controlled variables, and briefly outline four tests.

Using what they have learned in the bubble gum experiment, students choose from a list of questions to develop another experiment to conduct and are assessed based on their use of the scientific method.

- Which type of air freshener lasts longest?
- Which mouthwash works best?
- Which bubble bath makes the most bubbles?
- Which freezes in less time, cold water or hot water?
- Which paper towels are most absorbent?
- What gets your heart pumping faster—climbing up and down stairs or using a stair-climbing machine?
- How can you keep the cat off a bed?
- Does sunlight fade the ink and paper in books and magazines?
- Can plants grow in artificial lights?
- What's the best way to keep the hallway rug from slipping?
- Which floor cleaner gives the most shine?

- Which brand of popcorn pops best?
- What substance is best for melting snow and ice in the driveway?
- Does water boil at the same temperature every day?
- What dish washing soap cleans best?

The Assessment

Students are given points according to the following criteria:

1. Observations, Predictions, and Inferences

- Make sense (2 points)
- Relate to topic (3 points)

2. Investigative Question

- Appropriate; stated in a manner that suggests experimentation (2 points)

3. Hypothesis

- Educated, testable; demonstrates cause and effect (5 points)

4. Experiment

- Manipulated variable identified (2 points)
- Controlled variables identified (3 points)
- Procedure detailed and thoughtful (can be duplicated) (5 points)
- Data accurate and appropriate (5 points)
- Data in organized display (table, graph, chart) (5 points)

5. Conclusion

- Clear and well-stated; addresses validity of hypothesis; identifies areas of possible concern (5 points)

6. Overall

- Changes and recommendations provided (3 points)
- Written neatly and clearly (10 points)

Assessing Naturalist Intelligence

Naturalist assessments ask students to demonstrate their learning and understanding in and through the natural world and natural environment around us. The primary mode of this type of assessment is the recognition, appreciation, and comprehension of a variety of patterns and designs as they show up in the flora and fauna of nature.

Naturalist assessments should require students to recognize natural groupings, chart natural patterns, know and commune with the natural world, distinguish among and classify members of a species, and discern neighboring species. Students must be able to demonstrate their understanding, learning, and knowledge by using or incorporating objects and processes from or in the natural world, by interacting with nature (as in an experiment or growing something), by making accurate observations about nature and drawing conclusions from such observations.

Guidelines for Creating Naturalist Rubrics

When you assess students using the naturalist intelligence, you challenge them to prove their understanding of certain curricular concepts in naturalist ways. You must always look for this conceptual understanding in and through whatever they have produced.

Remember, you are not assessing their so-called "scientific ability." Your main concern is with the cognitive process, the unique way of knowing, represented by the naturalist intelligence. The knowing that occurs in the naturalist intelligence is embodied in the human interest, recognition, understanding, and appreciation of the natural world, including various classifications of plants, animals, and insects; sensitivity to various natural phenomena, such as weather patterns, flowing water, and rock formations; and a high regard for the natural environment. This intelligence must involve direct or indirect contact and involvement with nature. The key is to learn to "read" and interpret the naturalist representations for students' actual understanding of the material being assessed.

Sample Rubrics for Naturalist Intelligence

▶ Hands-on Labs and Demonstrations

Performing various natural experiments or activities that demonstrate understanding of specific concepts, topics, or subjects

INTELLIGENCE PERFORMANCE

Basic-Level Rubric

- One-on-one demonstrations that match or reproduce exactly experiments already performed

Complex-Level Rubric

- Extended experiments that are based on and utilize past experiments but move to new areas of inquiry

Higher-Order Rubric

- New and creative experiments in which student's own hypotheses, ideas, and interests are examined

CONTENT UNDERSTANDING

Questions to Ask Myself

- Do I sense the student is understanding the experiment?
- Does the student grasp the point and purpose of the experiment?
- Does the student understand the importance of the experiment and what is being learned through the experiment?

Questions to Ask Students

- "Please walk me through the steps of the experiment, explaining why you do each step."
- "If you had to tell someone who has not studied this material why this experiment is important, what would you say?"
- "Explain other ways you could use this experiment to test other things."

▶ # Species and Natural Pattern Classification

Using various classification matrices to show understanding

INTELLIGENCE PERFORMANCE

Basic-Level Rubric

- Identifies and recognizes very obvious patterns and categories

Complex-Level Rubric

- Sees unusual patterns that are not obvious; creates categories that demonstrate subtleties in groupings

Higher-Order Rubric

- Discerns new patterns of connection and relationships between the natural world and the human-created world

CONTENT UNDERSTANDING

Questions to Ask Myself

- Does the student accurately perceive the natural patterns and classify them?
- What do I see in the work that makes me think the student understands, even though I am confused by the classification?
- Where has the student gone beyond what I was expecting so that I need an explanation?

Questions to Ask Students

- "Explain why you grouped things the way you did and why you chose these categories."
- "Please help me understand the patterns you have sensed and how you are classifying them."
- "What other natural patterns occur to you that could fit in your categories?"

▶ Nature Encounters and Field Trips

Using firsthand nature experiences or bringing nature in via videos, objects, animals, and plants to demonstrate understanding

INTELLIGENCE PERFORMANCE

Basic-Level Rubric

- Uses and incorporates obvious items from the natural world

Complex-Level Rubric

- Uses the natural world in unusual and creative ways to prove understanding

Higher-Order Rubric

- Employs items in the natural world to create analogies between the natural world and the material being assessed

CONTENT UNDERSTANDING

Questions to Ask Myself

- Where do I sense some special connection or appreciation for the natural world that I need to discuss?
- What do I see that leads me to think the student understands more than the project or report shows?
- Where do the observations and conclusions seem somewhat askew, requiring me to probe for further understanding?

Questions to Ask Students

- "I'm not sure I understand what you saw that led you to this conclusion. Please tell me more."
- "I think you learned more on the field trip than you have expressed here. Can you tell me about it?"
- "How would explain what you have learned here to your parents or a friend in another class?"

Environmental Feedback

Employing natural, auditory, olfactory, visual, and gustatory feedback coming from the natural environment to show a grasp of material

INTELLIGENCE PERFORMANCE

Basic-Level Rubric

- Uses and responds to only the most obvious environmental inputs (that is, a one-to-one relationship)

Complex-Level Rubric

- Makes unexpected connections with the sounds, smells, sights, and tastes from the environment and uses these in creative ways

Higher-Order Rubric

- Senses subtle and profound relationships and connections between the environmental inputs and own being

CONTENT UNDERSTANDING

Questions to Ask Myself

- Does the student accurately perceive and understand the sensory input?
- Where has the student gone beyond the obvious feedback to perceive more subtle inputs?
- Where is there a mismatch between inputs the student is using and content?

Questions to Ask Students

- "Why did you associate those inputs with those concepts? What was your thinking?"
- "What was the process you used to go beyond the obvious feedback to sense these other things?"
- "Experience this feedback again and pay close attention. What do you hear? See? Smell?

▶ Nature Observations

Participating in activities such as bird-watching, noting geological differences, keeping nature journals to demonstrate learning

INTELLIGENCE PERFORMANCE

Basic-Level Rubric

■ Notices the most obvious, surface aspects of the natural setting being explored

Complex-Level Rubric

■ Makes observations that move beyond the obvious; raises questions about what is being observed

Higher-Order Rubric

■ Makes creative leaps in observation and conclusions drawn; grasps many connections between the observations and the concepts being assessed

CONTENT UNDERSTANDING

Questions to Ask Myself

■ What observations beyond what I was anticipating has the student made?

■ What obvious natural things did the student seem to miss or misunderstand?

■ Do the conclusions the student draws from the observations make sense? What is the student learning from the observations?

Questions to Ask Students

■ "Why did you draw these conclusions from what you observed? Please help me see the connections you saw."

■ "Please share the full observation process you used that led you to come up with these conclusions."

■ "It seems that you missed a lot. What could you do to 'hone' your observation skills so you'd see more?"

Caring for Plants and Animals

Growing and caring for plants or raising animals as a way to show comprehension of various concepts

INTELLIGENCE PERFORMANCE

Basic-Level Rubric

- Project is fairly simple; student has simply followed the expected steps for growing something or caring for an animal

Complex-Level Rubric

- Project shows real thoughtfulness in design and care in presentation; goes beyond expected steps to create something new

Higher-Order Rubric

- Project shows an almost empathetic understanding of and relationship to plants and animals

CONTENT UNDERSTANDING

Questions to Ask Myself

- What in the plant and animal projects seems to show a profound understanding of the material?
- Where does the student fail to make connections between the project and the skills or content?
- What do I see in the project that either surprises me or confuses me and therefore requires further conversation?

Questions to Ask Students

- "Please explain what this project has to do with *x*."
- "I'm not sure I understand this part of your project. Please help me understand what you understand."
- "What other things did this project bring to mind that you would like to investigate?"

▶ Sensory Stimulation Exercises

Using sensory-based exposure to participate in nature's sounds, smells, tastes, touches, and sights to prove one's learning

INTELLIGENCE PERFORMANCE

Basic-Level Rubric

- Uses the obvious senses that one would expect to be associated with a given environment

Complex-Level Rubric

- Uses not-so-obvious, more subtle sensory stimulation possibilities of an environment

Higher-Order Rubric

- Combines and integrates the sounds, sights, smells, textures, tastes to create a nature art form

CONTENT UNDERSTANDING

Questions to Ask Myself

- As I observe the student's sensory relation to nature, where do I sense a deeper learning or knowing than what is being expressed?
- Where has the student used the senses and nature in very creative or unusual ways to show learning?
- Where does the student use the sensory information in ways that are somehow mismatched or out of sync?

Questions to Ask Students

- "I feel you know more or have learned more than this exercise let you express. Please tell me about it."
- "What made you decide to use these things from nature in the ways you did? Please tell me about your thinking."
- "What additional stimulants could you include to demonstrate your learning and understanding?"

▶ Conservation Practices

Participating in various learning projects to care for and preserve the natural environment

INTELLIGENCE PERFORMANCE

Basic-Level Rubric

■ Demonstrates a simple following of stated and agreed-on conservation guidelines and principles

Complex-Level Rubric

■ Shows an understanding of the spirit of conservation by performing related conservation practices that include but go beyond the guidelines

Higher-Order Rubric

■ Demonstrates an "at-home-ness" or unity with conserving the natural world because "It is me!"

CONTENT UNDERSTANDING

Questions to Ask Myself

■ What do I see in the project that shows a profound level of understanding?

■ Where do I see opportunities to take this student to new levels of understanding in and through the projects?

■ Where do I feel that this student is not understanding the material?

Questions to Ask Students

■ "You have demonstrated remarkable empathy in this project. What did you feel as you were doing it?"

■ "What if you had tried doing x here instead of y? What might have been the results?"

■ "I'm not sure why you chose to do x at this point in the project. Please explain it to me."

▶ Archetypal Pattern Recognition

Showing awareness of the many repeating patterns and designs in nature that manifest themselves throughout the universe

INTELLIGENCE PERFORMANCE

Basic-Level Rubric

- Recognizes the most obvious patterns previously pointed out by other people

Complex-Level Rubric

- Senses the obvious and patterns learned from others, but goes beyond to find new patterns

Higher-Order Rubric

- Grasps connections within connections and sees patterns within patterns, almost in a spiritual manner

CONTENT UNDERSTANDING

Questions to Ask Myself

- What patterns that the student has seen totally surprise me? What patterns is the student missing?
- Where do I sense a learning beyond what the student is expressing?
- What confuses me about what the student has seen?

Questions to Ask Students

- "I don't think I understand the patterns you have seen and how you interpreted them. Please help me."
- "What was the process you used to come up with these patterns?"
- "What have you learned about yourself and our world in and through these patterns?"

Natural World Simulations

Creating projects, such as dioramas, montages, photographs, drawings, and nature rubbings, that re-create or represent nature in some form

INTELLIGENCE PERFORMANCE

Basic-Level Rubric

- Simulation presents a literal representation of the basic facts, concepts, processes, or material

Complex-Level Rubric

- Simulation interprets meanings and implications of the facts and figures of the concepts

Higher-Order Rubric

- Simulation shows personal connections to the material through abstract, symbolic, or metaphorical representations

CONTENT UNDERSTANDING

Questions to Ask Myself

- Does the simulation accurately represent the information?
- What do I see that demonstrates a thorough understanding of the material?
- Where am I having trouble understanding a simulation's relationship to the material?

Questions to Ask Students

- "I think I understand these parts of your simulation, but can you help me understand these?"
- "Why did you decide to represent your learning in this way? What was your thinking?"
- "What additional things from the natural environment could you have used?"

Naturalist Examples

The information about the naturalist intelligence is so new, at least when added to that of the original seven intelligences, that I received no sample lessons or assessments that used this intelligence. Following are several of my own examples that show how the naturalist intelligence could be used in various curricular areas. However, I did not develop rubrics for them. Unlike the other examples in this section, these are untested in the classroom, but in my mind's eye, they have been tested *virtually*. I hope some of you will take these ideas and the naturalist rubrics and create examples, test them in your classrooms, and share them at a later time.

Language Arts Activity

Write poetry, a descriptive essay, or a story to re-create an important nature experience you have had or re-create the experience by speaking into a tape recorder. Present your writing or speaking to the class.

Mathematics Activity

Take a walk outside with a partner and see how much math you can find in nature. Look for geometric shapes. Look for various number patterns that occur naturally. Where do you see addition, subtraction, division, and multiplication taking place? Where do you see fractions? With your partner, create a math problem for the class to solve based on your observations.

Science and Health Activity

Keep a diary in which you record the natural processes, patterns, and dynamics of your own body. Then compare and contrast the entries with the corresponding processes, patterns, and dynamics in a favorite pet or another animal. Create a display that reports your findings.

Global Studies and Geography Activity

Create a multimedia experiential report on the natural environments of a culture. The report must be highly sensory in that it will give others the experience of tasting, touching, feeling, smelling, seeing, and so on elements of the natural world that shaped the culture. Present your report to the class.

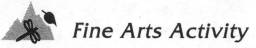

History Activity

Study and understand how natural events have influenced, shaped, and in some cases, determined historical direction. Consider contemporary and historical examples. Create a PBS-style video of your findings. You may use the Internet or a photograph and picture gallery.

Fine Arts Activity

Use sounds, rhythms, beats, music, and vibrations from the natural environment to compose and record an auditory piece. No humanmade sounds allowed. The composition should have three movements and incorporate a wide range of natural sounds. Present your audiotape to the class.

5
Object-Free Intelligences
Musical-Rhythmic and Verbal-Linguistic

Performance Rubrics

In Howard Gardner's 1983 grouping of the intelligences, verbal-linguistic and musical-rhythmic fall under the category "object free." Gardner notes that the "'object-free' forms . . . are not fashioned or channeled by the physical world but, instead, reflect the structures of particular languages and music. They may also reflect features of the auditory and oral systems, though . . . language and music may each develop, at least to some extent, in the absence of these sensory modalities" (2).

Unlike the object-related intelligences, the object-free intelligences do not rely on objects, real or imagined, that have an independent existence in the external world or the world of the imagination. Think for a moment about what an author can create via the written word, whether or not there are actual physical objects that correspond to the writing. Through the medium of language we can journey to realms of fantasy or we can encounter people and creatures we will never meet in so-called "real life." This phenomenon is even more obvious in the musical-rhythmic (auditory-vibrational) intelligence where we are totally immersed in a realm, not of concrete objects, but of sound, vibration, tones, beats, and so on.

We are dealing with how an intelligence expresses its knowing. When working with the verbal-linguistic and musical-rhythmic intelligences, you must crawl inside their unique world and open yourself to processing information within these unique language systems, which are not based on concrete stuff that you can taste, touch, smell, and see. In order to create fair assessments and rubrics that utilize these two intelligences, we must be firmly rooted in the power of language to create reality and in the evocative realms of sound and vibration.

Musical-Rhythmic Intelligence

In my work I have started to call this intelligence the auditory-vibrational intelligence, for I believe that, while music and rhythm are certainly part of this intelligence, it is not limited only to musical and rhythmic capacities. We are immersed in the whole realm of sound and vibration that involves sounds and vibrations from the natural and human-created environment, sounds and vibrations from machines, sounds and vibrations from musical and percussion instruments, and sounds and vibrations produced by the human vocal chords.

In some ways the consciousness-altering effects of music, rhythm, sound, and vibration are more powerful than the elements of any other intelligence. Just think of their power to shift our moods, inspire religious devotion, evoke national pride, express deep love for another or deep loss and grief. Consider the power of music, rhythm, sound, and vibration when you are watching a TV show or a movie—the score and sound track are used to anticipate what will happen next or to enhance the action in a particular scene. I have also been fascinated with the development of this auditory-vibrational intelligence in people who are profoundly deaf. Often their capacities to "hear" through vibrational patterns have developed to very high levels of cognitive processing.

Verbal-Linguistic Intelligence

The verbal-linguistic intelligence deals with the mystery, complexity, and power of the written and spoken word. It involves understanding individual meanings (semantics), order within a larger context of other words (syntax), meanings within various social and cultural contexts (praxis), and sounds of the spoken word spoken (phonetics), again, individually and as they are linked with other words. Just think how powerful words can be: They can evoke emotion. They can move people to action. They can make us laugh. They can produce feelings of hatred. They can heal.

One interesting (and challenging!) thing about the verbal-linguistic intelligence is that a person may be strong and proficient in using and delivering the spoken word while less than proficient in using the written word and vice versa. Even with the spoken and written word, a person may have various levels of proficiency; for example, the ability to write beautiful and flowing poetry but the inability to write a clear, logical paragraph. Or the ability to deliver a rousing persuasive speech but the inability to deliver a coherent set of step-by-step instructions.

When we consider these object-free intelligences and the task of using them to assess students, we must remember that the assessments must be couched in the cognitive frameworks of these intelligences; students must be required to work in much more abstract realms than when they are working with concrete objects. Thus the instruments you will be using involve all the subtle nuances of the most complex (and potentially abstract) symbol systems humanity has created—namely, language and multitudinous, gross and subtle, dimensions of sound, vibration, music, and rhythm. The suggested instruments were designed to help us root ourselves within the unique cognitive reality of verbal-linguistic and musical-rhythmic intelligences by requiring us to work with their unique media and within their language systems.

Assessing Musical-Rhythmic (Auditory-Vibrational) Intelligence

Musical-rhythmic intelligence assessments ask students to demonstrate their knowledge and learning through hearing, responding to, and creating sound. The primary mode of these assessments is tonal and rhythmic patterns, including sounds produced with the human vocal chords and the body, sounds in the environment (including both natural and otherwise), sounds from musical and percussion instruments ("live" as well as on the radio, CDs, and audiocassette tapes), and sounds produced by different kinds of machines (for example, road construction vehicles, office electronic/computer equipment).

Musical-rhythmic assessments should require students to appreciate the structure of music and rhythm, become aware of the schema or frames for hearing music and rhythm, become sensitive to the qualities of various sounds (including such things as pitch, timbre, tempo, and tone), create and reproduce melody and rhythm, and express thoughts, feelings, ideas, and emotions through tonal, vibrational, and rhythmic patterns. On the one hand, students must be able to show understanding through the recognition of various types of music, rhythms, or other meaningful sounds and be able to associate or connect this music, rhythm, and sound to what is being assessed; on the other hand, they must able to produce music, rhythm, and sound to illustrate or represent their understanding.

Guidelines for Creating Musical-Rhythmic Content Rubrics

When you assess students using musical-rhythmic intelligence, you challenge them to prove their understanding of certain curricular concepts using such things as sound, rhythm, tones, vibrational patterns, music, beats, varying pitches, pacing, and so on. You must always look for this conceptual understanding in and through what they have produced. You must look for direct and indirect expressions of associations and relationships among concepts and the sound, rhythm, music, and vibrations they employ and create. You must look for various "auditory analogies" they have created. Remember, you are not concerned with their so-called "musical ability." Being able to carry a tune or having a good sense of rhythm has little to do with musical-rhythmic intelligence in the first instance. Musical-rhythmic intelligence is a way of knowing, understanding, and learning that occurs through the whole realm of sound and vibration. Your main concern is the cognitive process, the unique way of knowing represented by the musical-rhythmic product. The key is to learn to "read" and interpret these musical-rhythmic (auditory-vibrational) representations for students' actual understanding of the material being assessed.

Sample Rubrics for Musical-Rhythmic Intelligence

 ## Creating Concept Songs and Raps

Creating songs or raps that demonstrate understanding of certain concepts, ideas, or processes

INTELLIGENCE PERFORMANCE

Basic-Level Rubric

- Song or rap involves simple substitutions of factual information in an existing composition

Complex-Level Rubric

- Song or rap uses an existing piece to present information and understanding in a creative and original way

Higher-Order Rubric

- Song or rap is an original creation that demonstrates thorough understanding of the concepts, ideas, or processes

CONTENT UNDERSTANDING

Questions to Ask Myself

- Does the song or rap include accurate, required information?
- Where has the song or rap gone beyond just the facts to demonstrate an understanding of the facts—why they're important, how to apply them, and so on?
- What parts of the song or rap lead me to believe the student understands more than what's expressed?

Questions to Ask Students

- "These parts of your song or rap aren't quite on target. How could you change it to be more accurate?"
- "Tell me more about what you were expressing in your presentation."
- "How would your song or rap change if you wanted someone who has not studied these ideas to understand them?"

Illustrating with Sound

Making sounds that are appropriate to and suggestive of certain concepts

INTELLIGENCE PERFORMANCE

Basic-Level Rubric

- Uses obvious, expected, single-dimension sounds to suggest certain concepts

Complex-Level Rubric

- Employs an array of interesting, creative sounds that are suggestive of the information or concepts

Higher-Order Rubric

- Uses multiple sounds to create an "auditory mirror" or "auditory reflection" of the information

CONTENT UNDERSTANDING

Questions to Ask Myself

- Where are the sound illustrations on target and where does there seem to be a mismatch?
- What about the illustration really surprises or intrigues me, or makes me want to know more?
- Where do I feel that they could further reveal their understanding by expanding on the sound illustrations?

Questions to Ask Students

- "I understand how certain of the sounds you have used illustrate the concepts, but please explain these."
- "I like the sounds you chose to illustrate the various concepts. If you had to add seven more sounds, what would you add and why?"
- "Please take me inside what you were thinking and feeling as you created your sound illustration. Why did you choose each sound?"

Discerning Rhythmic Patterns

Recognizing various rhythms, beats, and vibrations as they relate to concepts

INTELLIGENCE PERFORMANCE

Basic-Level Rubric

- Senses unmistakable, one-on-one beats, vibrations, and rhythms

Complex-Level Rubric

- Senses multiple dimensions and possibilities of beats, vibrations, and rhythms

Higher-Order Rubric

- Senses subtle, not obvious relationships among beats, vibrations, and rhythms

CONTENT UNDERSTANDING

Questions to Ask Myself

- Where is the student seeing clear, unmistakable, and obvious relationships among the rhythmic patterns and the content?
- Where does the student seem confused or uncertain about how the rhythmic patterns created or employed relate to the topics?
- Where do I sense a profound understanding between the concepts and the rhythms, beats, and vibrations?

Questions to Ask Students

- "Please explain how these beats relate to what we've been studying."
- "I'm fascinated by how you connected the rhythmic patterns with the content. How did you do it? What were you thinking?"
- "If you were going to create additional rhythmic patterns to express these ideas, what beats or rhythms would you make?"

Composing a Sound Track

Creating musical patterns and melody to accompany various concepts, processes, or ideas

INTELLIGENCE PERFORMANCE

Basic-Level Rubric

- Employs simple composition techniques with music, rhythm, and sound created by someone else

Complex-Level Rubric

- Combines original music, rhythm, and sound with those created by someone else to create concept-appropriate accompaniment

Higher-Order Rubric

- Creates a seamless concept sound track that orchestrates original and other-created music, rhythm, and sound

CONTENT UNDERSTANDING

Questions to Ask Myself

- Where does the student's composition demonstrate clear understanding?
- Where is the connection between the composition and concepts not obvious, but I intuit the student understands?
- Where am I overwhelmed by the composition and want to know more about their thinking and their creative process?

Questions to Ask Students

- "What about these concepts and these musical patterns and melodies made you decide to put them together?"
- "I think I understand these aspects of your composition, but please explain how these are related to the topic."
- "How would you adapt you composition if you were going to teach a younger child these concepts?"

Linking Music and Rhythm with Concepts

Relating existing musical-rhythmic compositions to concepts, processes, or ideas

INTELLIGENCE PERFORMANCE

Basic-Level Rubric
- Uses obvious, expected, literal links with the material (for example, study of rural America and "The Farmer in the Dell")

Complex-Level Rubric
- Makes unusual, surprising, and unexpected links (for example, study of rural America and "People")

Higher-Order Rubric
- Discovers or creates new links between the subject matter and existing compositions (for example, rural America and "Where Have All the Flowers Gone?")

CONTENT UNDERSTANDING

Questions to Ask Myself
- Where am I delighted and surprised by the links made between the concepts and certain pieces of music and rhythm?
- Where do the links seem to be too remote or somehow miss the mark?
- About what links do I feel I need to ask questions to capture a deeper understanding?

Questions to Ask Students
- "Please explain each of the links you have made, telling how each is appropriate and why you chose a certain piece of music or rhythm."
- "I don't understand how this piece goes with these concepts. Please help me understand your thinking."
- "How did you move from the concepts we've been studying to the ingenious links you have made to other things?"

Orchestrating Music and Rhythm

Illustrating understanding of concepts through such techniques as volume, timing, timbre, pacing of rhythmic patterns, and tonal qualities

INTELLIGENCE PERFORMANCE

Basic-Level Rubric

- Effective use of one or two of the techniques to show understanding

Complex-Level Rubric

- Effective use of each technique in turn to demonstrate understanding

Higher-Order Rubric

- Effective simultaneous use of techniques to create a multidimensional, auditory illustration

CONTENT UNDERSTANDING

Questions to Ask Myself

- Where do I sense clear connections and understandings between the performance and the concepts?
- What uses of orchestration techniques do I need to question to discover how they relate to the information?
- Where do I get a feeling of integrated flow of the musical orchestration and the flow of the concepts or processes?

Questions to Ask Students

- "Please help me understand what was in your mind when you decided to use these orchestration techniques in conjunction with these concepts."
- "If you were going to make a recording of your presentation, what title would you give it and what would be on the CD jacket cover?"
- "Please explain your thinking and feelings about each section or movement of your piece."

▶ Recognizing Tonal Patterns and Qualities

Recognizing relevant tonal patterns that are related to specific topics

INTELLIGENCE PERFORMANCE

Basic-Level Rubric
- Immediate recognition of obvious, isolated tones or sounds when connected with specific topics

Complex-Level Rubric
- Recognition of relevant tones and sounds in the midst of other, unrelated tones and sounds

Higher-Order Rubric
- Recognition of tonal patterns that lead to imagining of other tones and sounds relevant to the topic

CONTENT UNDERSTANDING

Questions to Ask Myself
- At what points did the student instantly recognize, and easily and quickly make curricular connections with, the tonal patterns and qualities?
- What tonal patterns were less obvious or did not seem to fit with the concepts?
- Where did I sense that the student was not only connecting the tonal patterns and the curriculum but sensing other tonal patterns and qualities that could be used?

Questions to Ask Students
- "You seemed to make very certain connections between the tonal patterns and the content. Please explain more about this to me."
- "Why did you have difficulty seeing the relationship between these tonal patterns and the concepts we've been studying?"
- "What other associations and connections were you making between the tonal patterns and what we've been studying?"

Creating Percussion Patterns

Using various kinds of vibrations and beats to communicate information or understanding

INTELLIGENCE PERFORMANCE

Basic-Level Rubric

- Simple, to-be-expected beats and vibrations connected to their obvious counterparts

Complex-Level Rubric

- Unusual and surprising percussion patterns employed in creative ways to demonstrate understanding

Higher-Order Rubric

- Use of a wide range of beats and vibrational patterns to communicate the essence of a concept, process, or idea

CONTENT UNDERSTANDING

Questions to Ask Myself

- Where do the beats and vibrational patterns mirror the concepts or processes?
- Where am I confused or uncertain about what the percussion patterns are meant to express?
- Where has the student gone beyond anything I expected and shown me a thorough understanding of the content through beat and vibration?

Questions to Ask Students

- "Please show me how each of the percussion patterns you have used relates to what we've been studying."
- "Please take me inside your thinking process. How did you come up with this percussional expression for these concepts?"
- "If you had to add some words or phrases to your patterns, what would they be?"

▶ Analyzing Musical Structures

Sensing and explaining connections among various musical forms and concepts

INTELLIGENCE PERFORMANCE

Basic-Level Rubric

- Simple recognition of a connection between a musical form and a concept (for example, Gregorian chant and the Middle Ages)

Complex-Level Rubric

- Understanding of several, beyond the obvious connections between musical forms and a concept (for example, ways folk music shaped the 1970s)

Higher-Order Rubric

- Creation of powerful analogies among various musical forms or structures and concepts (for example, using 3/4 time to understand genetic transformations)

CONTENT UNDERSTANDING

Questions to Ask Myself

- Where does the student grasp and understand the relationships among various musical forms and types and the content?
- Where could I help the student grasp and understand some of the more subtle aspects of the subject through the musical forms?
- At what points is the student seeing no connections or making confusing connections?

Questions to Ask Students

- "Let's analyze this type of music. Can you see any relationships between this and our subject matter?"
- "Please explain how this musical form made you make the connections and associations you made."
- "What other types of music might you use to understand these concepts? Why and how are they appropriate?"

▶ Reproducing Musical, Rhythmic, and Auditory Patterns

Exhibiting understanding through replication of music, rhythm, and sound

INTELLIGENCE PERFORMANCE

Basic-Level Rubric

- Exact mimicking of music, rhythms, and sounds that relate to a specific concept

Complex-Level Rubric

- Addition of own interpretive auditory embellishments to mimicking of appropriate music, rhythm, and sounds

Higher-Order Rubric

- Appropriate music, rhythms, and sounds of one topic lead to linking music, rhythm, and sounds from another topic or subject area

CONTENT UNDERSTANDING

Questions to Ask Myself

- Are the sounds, music, and rhythm clearly and appropriately related to the topic?
- Where do I fail to see the relationship between the sounds, music, and rhythm and the content?
- What really caught me off guard by its cleverness and makes me want to have the student explain more fully?

Questions to Ask Students

- "I don't see the relationship between the sounds, music, and rhythm you used and the concepts. Please help me see what you have seen."
- "What made you choose these particular sounds, music, or rhythms to go with these particular concepts? Why do you feel they fit?"
- "Please take me through the process or steps you used to create these sound representations to accompany these concepts."

Musical-Rhythmic Teacher Examples

Cell-abrate with Song

This example comes from Michelle Jansky. The lesson and assessment involve students in the creation of a song to demonstrate their understanding of the parts and functions of cells. While not precisely a rubric, the articulation of the criteria for the song is clear. Students are assessed primarily on whether they have included all the facts in their song. From the perspective of a junior high student, probably the most difficult part of the grading is that all group members sing—however, the criterion is not "sing well" or even "sing on key"! When you look at the grade report, you see no mention of musical ability. This lesson is an excellent example of the use of musical-rhythmic intelligence as a mnemonic device to aid memory and understanding.

The Activity

Students are placed in groups and are given the following guidelines by which to collaborate on a song:

1. The song must have an *appropriate title*.
2. Song must include *definition of a cell*.
3. Plant cell songs must define or describe the following parts:

cell wall	*chloroplast*
cell membrane	*vacuole*
nucleus	*mitochondria*
cytoplasm	*golgi body*

   Animal cell songs must define or describe the following parts:

cell membrane	*mitochondria*
nucleus	*endoplasmic reticulum*
cytoplasm	*ribosome*
vacuole	*golgi body*

They must include all the parts to get the maximum possible points. The entire group sings the song for the class. They must also turn in a neatly written, typed, or word processed copy of their songs in verse form.

The Assessment

Students are given points for appearance of the written song and correct spelling (4 possible points), title (2 points), definition of *cell* (2 points), each cell structure they include (up to 8 points), and the participation of all group members in singing the song (4 points).

Performing Patterns with Rhythm

The following example is from the Eureka Project, which is an integration project that is sponsored by the Halton Board of Education in Toronto, Ontario. The developers articulated several results they expected from Eureka: to help students understand their intelligences, to teach ways to express oneself and one's learning using various intelligences, to know ways to use multiple intelligences to effect lifelong learning and make career choices, and to recognize one's and others' intelligence strengths and areas that need growth. The Eureka project was my initial inspiration for writing this book. The rubrics in this activity are closer to the kinds of things I have presented in this book than are the other examples.

The unit emphasizes the auditory-vibrational aspects of the intelligence; that is, the unit works more with the realm of natural and human-created sounds than with music per se. The unit immediately immerses students in the realm of sound and vibration. This entry point is the most effective and quickest way to activate, stimulate, or trigger an intelligence in the brain-mind-body system. Students work with the tools and capacities of the intelligence; namely, they are producing sound, experimenting with rhythms and beats, and creating music. Again, such creation is the best way to enhance, strengthen, amplify, and grow an intelligence. Although the main emphasis of this unit is increasing students' musical-rhythmic intelligence capacities, it could very easily be extended, modified, and adapted to the more traditional academic units in such areas as language arts, history, science, mathematics, and so on.

The Activity

The activity is meant to help students develop an awareness of the musical-rhythmic intelligence, know how to create patterns in response to a beat, respond to the beat in music, and work cooperatively to create a routine. The teacher plays a few minutes of the music; students discover various ways they can move lummi sticks to the beat. Without music, students create a 4-beat pattern and perform the pattern to music. They create another 4-beat pattern to add on to their first and perform the 8-beat pattern. They repeat the process with contrasting music, for example, fast or slow, loud or soft, theme-oriented, dance, rock or country. You might also have students create 16- or 32-beat patterns.

In addition to the musical-rhythmic intelligence, students use the bodily-kinesthetic intelligence. They also develop cooperative group skills, and perception and concept-formation skills.

The Assessment

Students are assessed as undeveloped if they do not repeat the pattern on the beat, as developing if they begin to repeat the patterns on the beat, and as highly developed if they repeat the pattern consistently, changing as the tempo changes.

Sound Compositions

The comments from the previous activity, performing patterns with rhythm, apply to this example, as well.

The Activity

Students develop, identify, and sequence appropriate sounds for compositions. They organize, manipulate, and vary the musical elements into a composition and performance. They also demonstrate a sense of personal satisfaction when participating as a creator and performer of music. Students listen to examples of sound stories, such as *Saturday Morning, By Canoe at Loon Lake*. They record a sound and action sequence and the moods created, or take a sound walk and record sounds. In cooperative groups, students create sound stories with all available sound sources, for example, vocal, body (stamp, clap, snap), found sounds (rulers, desktops, paper, keys), taped sounds (natural, household), instrumental and untuned percussion (wood blocks, maracas), tuned percussion (xylophone), keyboards, and other musical instruments. They may use topics such as a trip to the zoo, getting ready for school, the rain forest, a day at the mall, or TV fast forward. They notate the score, devising any system the group suggests, then perform or record the composition. Students in the audience list the sequence of sounds and guess the title. For younger children, you might limit the stories to four sound sequences; older children might undertake a longer series.

In addition to the musical-rhythmic intelligence, students use the interpersonal intelligence. They also learn cooperative group roles, such as recorder, encourager, instrument gatherer, and time keeper.

The Assessment

Students' compositions are assessed as undeveloped if they do not sequence appropriate sounds, as developing if they begin to show sequencing, and as highly developed if the sounds are organized and appropriately sequenced. Students' performances are assessed as undeveloped if they do not perform the sound composition effectively, as developing if they begin to perform the composition with continuity and facility, and as highly developed if they perform with confidence and facility.

Assessing Verbal-Linguistic Intelligence

Verbal-linguistic assessments ask students to demonstrate their knowledge and learning through effective linguistic communication. The primary mode of this form of assessment is written and spoken language, including essays and reports, formal and impromptu speeches or conversation, dialogues, creative writing and poetry, and comprehension of reading.

Verbal-linguistic assessments require students to understand the order and meaning of words, convince someone to take a particular course of action (persuasive speaking), learn something from another's instructions and be able to teach someone by giving instructions, write humorous anecdotes and tell jokes, recall written or spoken information, and analyze metalinguistics (use of language to understand language itself). Students must be able to represent their learning and understanding in and through proper grammar, syntax, phonetics, and praxis of a formal language system.

Guidelines for Creating Verbal-Linguistic Content Rubrics

When you assess students using verbal-linguistic intelligence, you challenge them to prove their understanding of certain curricular concepts using all dimensions of the spoken and written language, including various methods or types of writing (narrative, comparison and contrast, anecdotal, interrogative), effective use of various forms of language (metaphor, similes, analogy, hyperbole, correct grammar, and so on), various types of formal and informal speech (casual conversation, persuasive speech, demonstration, informative speech, or inspirational speech), storytelling and story creation, linguistic humor (puns, jokes, limericks, and other "twists and turns" of the language), reading and comprehension, understanding and using various genres of literature, and writing poetry and appreciating someone else's poetry. As you read what students have written or listen to what they are speaking, always look for their understanding of the concepts you are assessing in and through what they have produced. You must not accidentally get "swept off your feet" by the student who is extremely good with words or despair over the student who is not. You must always probe for the deeper meanings of their words and for the actual understanding that may be hidden in their facility (or lack thereof) with language. Verbal-linguistic intelligence, just like each of the other intelligences, is a way of knowing, understanding, and learning that occurs in and through the use of language to communicate with others. Your focus should be on the cognitive process, the unique way of knowing, represented by verbal-linguistic intelligence. The key in assessment is to learn to "read" and interpret various verbal-linguistic representations for students' actual understanding of the material being assessed.

Sample Rubrics for Verbal-Linguistic Intelligence

▶ Essays

Using a variety of forms and sentence styles (declarative, interrogative, descriptive, and so on) to demonstrate one's knowledge

INTELLIGENCE PERFORMANCE

Basic-Level Rubric

- Utilizes one or two basic sentence forms throughout the essay to convey a simple understanding

Complex-Level Rubric

- Employs an interesting variety of writing forms and styles to show some wrestling with and digestion of the material

Higher-Order Rubric

- Bases essay clearly on the original material but uses a wide variety of writing techniques to express thoughts and feelings

CONTENT UNDERSTANDING

Questions to Ask Myself

- Where do I intuit the student knows more than she expressed?
- Where does it seem that the student missed the boat and I need to explore in other ways?
- Where am I blown away by the articulation and want to talk further about the insights?

Questions to Ask Students

- "I think you understand this material, but your writing doesn't communicate it. What other verbal ways could you demonstrate your learning?"
- "Please share with me the process you went through to create this essay."
- "If you had to write three more paragraphs to expand on and deepen your ideas, what would you write about?"

▶ Vocabulary Quizzes

Showing recognition and understanding of correct pronunciation and proper use of words

INTELLIGENCE PERFORMANCE

Basic-Level Rubric

- Recognizes words if presented in the same way as initially presented; uses words in expected, previously used ways

Complex-Level Rubric

- Identifies words in new contexts and is able to accurately use the words in new contexts

Higher-Order Rubric

- Incorporates the vocabulary into regular communication to express ideas and thoughts

CONTENT UNDERSTANDING

Questions to Ask Myself

- Where is the student using the new words correctly but I feel I need to explore his understanding of the larger meaning?
- Where is the student using the words in unusual and creative ways that indicate true understanding?
- Where is the student using the words in ways that indicate the words have become a part of her language repertoire?

Questions to Ask Students

- "What made you decide to use that word in that situation or context?"
- "If you had to express the meaning of that word using your own words, what would you say?"
- "How would you explain the meaning of that word to someone who could not read or understand the formal definition?"

Recall of Verbal Information

Using verbal games, puzzles, and question-and-answer activities to recall information

INTELLIGENCE PERFORMANCE

Basic-Level Rubric

- Recalled information is closely related to the learning situation or context

Complex-Level Rubric

- Recalled information is more remote from the first learning (for example, math facts in history or science)

Higher-Order Rubric

- Recalled information is used in meaningful and interesting ways that go beyond the context of the original learning

CONTENT UNDERSTANDING

Questions to Ask Myself

- Where is the student able to recognize and recall the information even when it is stated in ways different from those in the original learning?
- If the student gets stuck, do clues trigger the recall of the information?
- Where do I see the transfer of the information to a totally new context from that in which it was initially learned?

Questions to Ask Students

- "Think of other words you could use to express that information."
- "Think of at least five situations outside of school in which this information is useful."
- "What gimmicks can you use that will help you remember and be able to access this information when you need it?"

▶ Audiocassette Recordings

Recording the best answers, thoughts, intuitions, and related ideas

INTELLIGENCE PERFORMANCE

Basic-Level Rubric

- Recording is accurate and based wholly on the information previously studied and in the same form as originally studied

Complex-Level Rubric

- Recording presents several potentially "right" answers given various sets of circumstances

Higher-Order Rubric

- Recording articulates answers by proposing a variety of implications and applications

CONTENT UNDERSTANDING

Questions to Ask Myself

- What do I hear that leads me to believe the student knows and understands more?
- What is inaccurate?
- Where has the student gone beyond anything I expected?

Questions to Ask Students

- "If you had been able to include a video recording to go along with your spoken words, what would you have recorded?"
- "Let's talk about some things that were not really on target in your recording. How would you correct or change them?"
- "Please tell me about the creative process that led you to make this recording."

▶ # Poetry Writing

Expressing understanding in verse and through various kinds of rhyming patterns

INTELLIGENCE PERFORMANCE

Basic-Level Rubric

- Use of elementary rhyming or poetic rhythm patterns to express simple facts and figures

Complex-Level Rubric

- Use of a variety of techniques to demonstrate a thoughtful dialogue with the material

Higher-Order Rubric

- Use of poetry as a vehicle to express thoughts and feelings about and understanding of the material

CONTENT UNDERSTANDING

Questions to Ask Myself

- What metaphors or similes somewhat confuse me and require me to ask for clarification?
- What has the student expressed beautifully and makes me want to talk further?
- Has the student grasped the various techniques and used them to communicate his ideas and understanding effectively?

Questions to Ask Students

- "Please explain what you were trying to express when you used these metaphors or similes."
- "Why did you decide to use this technique to express your thoughts and feelings?"
- "Please take me inside your creative process and tell me how you created this poem."

▶ Linguistic Humor

Making jokes, riddles, and plays on words about various subjects and concepts

INTELLIGENCE PERFORMANCE

Basic-Level Rubric

■ Uses the most obvious, to-be-expected humor related exactly to the concepts

Complex-Level Rubric

■ Uses the material or concepts as a "jumping off" place for humorous talking or writing

Higher-Order Rubric

■ Creates an entire humorous routine based on the material and uses clever, witty language

CONTENT UNDERSTANDING

Questions to Ask Myself

■ Is the humor relevant, appropriate, and on target given the subject matter?

■ Where am I confused by the academic point being made?

■ What has the student produced that is almost "public performance funny" and that I want to discuss?

Questions to Ask Students

■ "I don't get it. Please help me see the humor and how it relates to the concepts."

■ "How did you come up with this routine? What was the process you went through to move from the academic content to this representation?"

■ "What is potentially funny about this material? What would be possible themes of a TV sitcom based on this?"

▶ Formal Speech

Making formal presentations, public speaking

INTELLIGENCE PERFORMANCE

Basic-Level Rubric

- Simple speech in which the basic facts, figures, and information are merely presented

Complex-Level Rubric

- Complex speech in which meanings are pondered and questions are raised

Higher-Order Rubric

- Complex speech in which the larger implications of the material and its connections to other learning and knowledge are explored

CONTENT UNDERSTANDING

Questions to Ask Myself

- Where did the student say something I sense wasn't meant, or where did the student fail to understand the full implications of something said?
- Where do I sense a fine articulation is hiding a less-than-adequate understanding?
- What makes me think the student understands a lot more than is put into words?

Questions to Ask Students

- "Please tell me more about what you meant when you said x."
- "I was blown away by your insight about x. Please tell me how you arrived at that conclusion."
- "I think you understand and know more than you talked about in your speech. How can I help you express this?"

▶ Cognitive Debates

Demonstrating knowledge of a subject by defending opinions or taking a side opposite to own opinions

INTELLIGENCE PERFORMANCE

Basic-Level Rubric

- Debate involves simple, one-dimensional arguments that present only one point of view

Complex Level Rubric

- Debate presents several points of view and contains clever support data for own point of view

Higher-Order Rubric

- Debate presents own point by taking on several opposing viewpoints and then showing why or how each is inadequate

CONTENT UNDERSTANDING

Questions to Ask Myself

- Where was the debating style great but the substance of the argument flimsy?
- Where was the style poor, but the arguments cogent and convincing?
- Where do I sense that the confrontational style of the debate hampered someone from revealing true understanding?

Questions to Ask Students

- "What other, more meaty points support the arguments than those you expressed in the debate?"
- "I don't think that you like debating. How else could you demonstrate your understanding of the material using verbal-linguistic intelligence?"
- "What were the main points you were expressing in the debate, whether or not they were winning arguments?"

Listening and Reporting

Listening to another's presentation, then reporting what was said and what was learned

INTELLIGENCE PERFORMANCE

Basic-Level Rubric

- Reports the most basic information that was communicated in the other's presentation

Complex-Level Rubric

- Reports the subtle aspects of the presentation and own conclusions drawn from the initial presentation

Higher-Order Rubric

- Demonstrates deep listening to and assimilation of the presentation by reporting own learning based on the initial presentation

CONTENT UNDERSTANDING

Questions to Ask Myself

- What leads me to believe that either the student wasn't listening or simply misunderstood what was reported?
- What information hidden between the lines did the student surprise me by picking up?
- Where did the student accurately hear and report on the presentation, but miss its implications or importance?

Questions to Ask Students

- "If you were going to make a new presentation entitled 'Why these concepts are important,' what are some points you would make?"
- "How did you get that information from that report?"
- "Let's go back to the original presentation. Can you remember what was actually said and what it means?"

▶ Learning Logs and Journals

Keeping a written or spoken record of the growth of knowledge and understanding

INTELLIGENCE PERFORMANCE

Basic-Level Rubric

- Journal or log records only the basic information and reports only superficial learning

Complex-Level Rubric

- Journal or log includes the affective impact of the material as well as some interpretation of its meaning

Higher-Order Rubric

- Journal or log is a profound statement of deep involvement with the material and discusses personal implications and applications

CONTENT UNDERSTANDING

Questions to Ask Myself

- What in the writing leads me to believe the student knows and understands more than has been expressed?
- Where do I see reflections that tell me the student misunderstands the information or material?
- What can I say or do that will deepen the learning expressed in the journal or log?

Questions to Ask Students

- "I have a feeling you have more to say on this topic. Can you tell me what else you've been thinking or feeling?"
- "What about this material led you to this reflection?"
- "What questions has this material raised for you? What other things would you find it interesting to explore?"

Verbal-Linguistic Teacher Examples

Art Criticism

The following example comes from Ann Krone. She includes a rubric for assessing critical reasoning in art criticism. (There is no lesson attached, but the lesson is clear.) The rubric evaluates many levels of what basically is a verbal-linguistic performance task. This rubric is an excellent example that objectifies many of the criteria we already use when we assess students' written work. I especially like the objective, clear descriptions of what constitutes a stage 1, 2, and 3 performance. These kinds of descriptions would not only help the teacher but would be extremely useful in giving students a picture of what a high-level performance looks like.

The Assessment

Stage 1 Performance

- Description (identifies things about the work that can be seen, named, and described): briefly names one or two objects—"There is a girl"; names and describes the obvious objects; makes a complete inventory of the subject matter and the elements and thoroughly describes them.

- Analysis: (1) Organization: identifies one or two elements—"I see wavy lines"; names and describes the elements and principles in the work; describes the dominant elements and principles and ways the artist uses them to reinforce the theme, meaning, mood, or feeling of the work. (2) Comparison of works of art: compares and contrasts the subject matter in two works of art.

- Interpretation (identifies the ideas, feelings, or moods communicated by the work of art): relates a personal response, that is, ideas, feelings, or moods—"It makes me sad."

- Evaluation (judges the quality or success of the work based on criteria): evaluates as "bad" or "good" because of personal feelings toward the subject matter.

Stage 2 Performance

- Description (identifies things about the work that can be seen, named, and described): names and describes the obvious objects.

- Analysis: (1) Organization: names and describes the elements and principles in the work. (2) Comparison of works of art: compares and contrasts the subject matter and composition of works.
- Interpretation (identifies ideas, feelings, or moods communicated by work): identifies the literal meaning.
- Evaluation (judges the quality or success of the work based on criteria): states an opinion and gives one reason for the opinion.

Stage 3 Performance

- Description (identifies things about the work that can be seen, named, and described): makes a complete descriptive inventory of the subject matter and elements.
- Analysis: (1) Organization: describes the dominant elements and principles and how the artist uses them to reinforce the theme, meaning, mood, or feeling. (2) Comparison of works of art: compares and contrasts with works across a range of cultures, and categories.
- Interpretation (identifies the ideas, feelings, or moods communicated by the work): forms a hypothesis about the symbolic or metaphorical meaning and substantiates the interpretation with evidence from the work.
- Evaluation (judges the quality or success of the work based on criteria): uses an aesthetic theory (imitation, expression, formal order, instrumental) to judge the work.

Social Studies Exam Rubric

Gloria Brudek sent the following rubric for a short-answer exam in social studies. The criteria help students understand up front that they are responsible for both content (understanding the region they are studying) and the quality of their writing (the essay itself). It is a relatively uncomplicated rubric to apply. The rubric is easily adaptable to almost any written work by simply plugging in various requirements for the content and writing mastery. In fact, the writing performance criteria could be spiraled to help students move to higher and better levels of writing as the year progresses.

The Activity

Students respond to the direction, "Write a paragraph that describes the region in which you live. Begin by first writing down the features of your region as discussed in class and in the text."

The Assessment

1. Top Notch:

The paragraph definitely describes five or more characteristics of the region: land forms, climate, and cultural information. It has a topic sentence with at least three good supporting sentences. It has descriptive and visual words. It is logical. It has correct grammar, spelling, punctuation, and capitalization.

2. Good:

The paragraph definitely describes four characteristics of the region: land forms, climate, and cultural information. Along with the topic sentence, it also has at least two supporting sentences, has descriptive and visual words, and is logical. Grammar, spelling, punctuation, and capitalization are used correctly most of the time.

3. Decent or Okay:

The paragraph describes three characteristics of the region: land forms, climate, and cultural information, although there is some inaccurate information in the paragraph. It has a topic sentence that is not clearly stated and lacks logical order. Some errors in grammar, spelling, punctuation, and capitalization occur.

4. Poor:

Only two characteristics of the region are described, and the paragraph has inaccurate information. The description is written illegibly and does not pertain to the region.

Written Research Report

The next example is courtesy of Mary Porter. It demonstrates a way to create complex rubrics that systematically move students to higher levels of understanding concepts as well as higher facility in expressing such understanding. The assignment is a written research report, but in principle, these same skills can easily be transferred to and integrated into formal speaking, as well. The main strength of the rubric is that students are given a crystal clear picture of what is involved to pursue a career; to complete the research project, they must experience the process itself. This example is one way to approach achieving assessment in context, which I spend a great deal of time talking about in this book.

The Activity

Students are required to research careers. They write a report on one career. The report must include a title page. The body of report must be at least two typed or word processed, double-spaced pages and include the following:

history of the occupation

educational requirements

tasks and responsibilities of position

required skills

required personal and physical characteristics

required work experience

required licensing or certification

working conditions

range of income

opportunities for advancement

job outlook

advantages and disadvantages

Students conclude by indicating why or why not the careers might be right for them. If they think the career is worth pursuing, they must indicate what they must do to prepare for it. They are also required to include a bibliography of at least three sources. They may include books, OCIS information, people, and other categories.

The Assessment

Students' reports are given an excellent rating (10 points) for each element in the above list that they treat completely. If they have 0 mistakes in grammar, spelling, paragraphing, sentence structure, and so on, they are rated excellent in these categories. Students' reports are given a skilled rating (5 points) for each element they treat incompletely. If they have one to three errors in spelling, grammar, and so on, they are rated skilled in these areas, as well. Students need help (0 points) in any element they do not cover at all. If they have four or more errors, they are rated as needing help in these areas, as well.

Written Research Report with Oral Presentation

The next example is courtesy of Mary Porter. The commentary on the previous example, Written Research Report, applies to this activity, as well. This assignment requires students to investigate and report on the process of buying a new or used car. Rubrics for the oral report are added.

The Activity

Students write a research paper that includes a complete description of a car, including model, year, options, and anything else that would affect the price. They tell from whom they got the information, a dealer or an individual seller. They include information about leases and loans. They also must deliver an oral report on their findings to the class.

The Assessment

Students are given 10 points (excellent) for each element they treat completely in their written and oral reports and for having zero errors. They are given 10 points for each of several overall elements, such as creativity, grammar and spelling, and report format. Students are given 5 points (skilled) for each element they treat incompletely in their reports and for having three or fewer errors. They are given 0 points for elements they did not do and for more than four errors.

Romeo and Juliet Research Report

The following rubric comes from Jean Hopkins (there is no activity description). It illustrates a way to use rubrics to encourage higher levels of performance in the intelligence and in content mastery. It provides guidelines Jean used for a research report on *Romeo and Juliet*. It lays out the verbal-linguistic criteria as well as the content mastery expected on a scale that ranges from 60 percent to 100 percent. I like both the clarity and straightforward approach of the rubrics as well as the relative ease with which one could simply redefine the criteria for various content areas as well as various performance skill levels. I am not a believer in using assessment as an external threat to students; namely, "If you don't do *x, y, z* according to *my* criteria you will suffer the consequences—a bad grade!" However, I believe that the way this example is constructed gives us a means to turn the rubric into an *intrinsic motivator* to improve performance, especially if students are involved in defining the criteria. If we can involve students in defining the various levels of performance, we enable them to set goals for themselves so they will be well inside what is necessary for a high-level performance.

The Assessment

1. Content

   - Novice: Less than two pages; sketchy; off topic
   - Experienced: At least two pages; basic; all on topic
   - Expert: Three or more pages; thorough information

2. Organization

- Confusing: No introduction or conclusion; no organization
- Readable: Basic introduction and conclusion; some order; no transitions
- Bestseller: Interesting introduction and conclusion; clear, logical order; transitions

3. Grammar

- Foreign Speaker: Frequent errors of all kinds
- Basic English Speaker: Some major errors, many minor errors
- English Professor: Few errors of any kind

4. Neatness

- In pencil with cross-outs; illegible; writing on back of paper; no headings
- In ink, only two cross-outs; legible; writing on back; name and date
- In ink, typed, or word processed; no cross-outs; legible; one side of paper; full heading

5. Bibliography

- Missing
- Included but poor form
- Included in good form

Spanish Homework

The following example comes from Jean Hopkins. It illustrates a way to use rubrics to encourage higher levels of performance in the intelligence and in content mastery. It provides guidelines Jean uses for Spanish homework. The comments included under the previous example, *Romeo and Juliet* Research Report, apply here as well.

The Assessment

Students are given percentage scores from 60 to 100 percent in each of five areas. Completeness is evaluated on how much the student completed (60 percent done = 60 percent in this category). Students receive a 60 percent in grammar if there are many errors of all kinds, a 70 percent if they have many errors but most are in new knowledge, an 80 percent if they have some errors in new knowledge, and a 90 to 100 percent if there are few errors of any kind. Accuracy of answers is determined by whether students made corrections and combined answers. Neatness ranges from illegible, messy, torn, or dirty at 60 percent to legible, organized, and clean at 90 to 100 percent. Effort ranges from "Well, you did turn in something" (60 percent) to "You kind of knew what to do" (70 percent) to "Okay, you did the right thing" (80 percent) to "You did your best!" (90 to 100 percent).

6
Personal Intelligences
Interpersonal and Intrapersonal _____

Performance Rubrics

The personal intelligences comprise the final group that Gardner (1993) delineated in his original research. He notes, "the personal forms of intelligence reflect a set of powerful and competing constraints: the existence of one's own person; the existence of other persons; the culture's presentations and interpretations of selves. There will be universal features of any sense of person or self, but also considerably cultural nuances, reflecting a host of historical and individuating factors" (334). At the heart of the inter- and intrapersonal intelligences are our own lives; our lives in relationship with one another and our lives as individuals. Gardner presents them in a single chapter to show that they are two parts of a related whole. Often, some of the greatest learning and discoveries about the self happen when we are working with or playing with others in some collaborative effort, be it a game, a community project, or a committee. The reverse is also true. Those things we discover about ourselves at the deepest levels of our being we can safely assume are also true about others; namely, once you get through the many layers of our personalities, you arrive at core selves in which there are many more similarities than differences!

In addition to the Janus-like nature of these intelligences, another factor makes them quite different from the other intelligences dealt with thus far. Inter- and intrapersonal intelligences tend to integrate and use all the intelligences as they go about their unique ways of knowing. Consider interpersonal intelligence and all that is involved when we are relating to or working with other people: We talk (verbal-linguistic). We use visual aids to enhance our meaning (visual-spatial). We gesture, make facial expressions and postures to enhance what we are trying to communicate (bodily-kinesthetic). The tone, pitch, and rhythm of our speech often communicate more than the meaning of the words we use (musical-rhythmic). And we follow certain logical rules in our use of language and in the act of communication itself (logical-mathematical). Now consider intrapersonal intelligence and the difficulty we often experience in adequately expressing the depth of our knowings about the self. To compensate we often resort to the world of symbols, which can help us point to the profound within our own lives. In other words, we give expression to our inner wrestlings, wisdom, and soul through art, drama, music, dance, poetry, and sculpture, or through seeking analogies and connections between our mundane daily lives and the archetypal patterns and powerful phenomena of the natural world.

Interpersonal Intelligence

This intelligence is the "stuff" of human relationships and relating, be it with one other person, as part of a team (or in some other type of cooperative effort), or in an informal gathering chatting with close friends in your living room. In some ways, the educational research into cooperative learning and how to make it work represents the state-of-the-art research on interpersonal intelligence. The very capacities that are at the core of this intelligence happen to be those very factors that cooperative learning researchers claim are key to successful learning groups: communicating effectively, doing one's part, listening to other points of view (even when I disagree!), respecting others' opinions, feeling empathy, being supportive, and so on.

One key finding of all cooperative learning research also supports a key factor for enhancing and strengthening this intelligence: we must explicitly teach students the social skills of cooperation and collaboration with others. The intelligence corollary is that we must consciously and diligently exercise and practice using the core capacities involved with interpersonal intelligence if we are to strengthen this intelligence within ourselves and our students. When we are using interpersonal intelligence as a focus in assessment, we must first involve students in great experiences of cooperative learning so that they will have a chance to exercise their interpersonal capacities. We can then build the assessments and rubrics on this experience of working with others.

Intrapersonal Intelligence

In some ways, intrapersonal intelligence is the most difficult of the intelligences to use to assess students' understanding. First, it is the most private of the intelligences and therefore much of its knowing resides in the inner realms of the self, which must somehow be objectified if we are to assess the intelligences. Second, intrapersonal intelligence is probably the most misunderstood of the intelligences; people often mistakenly assume that intrapersonal deals with religion or spirituality precisely because it involves the internal aspects of the self, such as feelings, beliefs, values, self-identity, questions and answers about life's meaning, goals, and so on. However, when we look squarely at the research behind this intelligence what we see is the cognitive, neurological, psychological process involved in any kind of serious introspection. A third difficulty is that this intelligence is not valued highly by our product-driven society; in other words, if you don't have some external thing to show for your efforts, you have wasted your time! The products that result from intrapersonal intelligence tend to be inner products and are sometimes difficult to communicate to someone else.

In the assessment tools and rubrics for working with intrapersonal intelligence, I attempt to provide a means for making external this inner world of the self. These kinds of instruments and the rubrics will benefit students in several ways: (1) They will foster a genuine self-reflectiveness. (2) They will help students find or create meaning in what they are studying (a critical part of deep learning and understanding). (3) They will force students to connect what they are learning to life beyond school.

The personal intelligences present us with some very interesting and exciting challenges when we use them to assess students' understanding. As with the other intelligences, it is important to remember that interpersonal and intrapersonal assessments must be couched in person-related frameworks. Students must be required to work with the socio- and psychological dynamics, capacities, and operations of the intelligences. The assessment instruments are designed to help us root ourselves firmly in the unique cognitive reality of interpersonal and intrapersonal intelligences by requiring us to work with the unique processes, dynamics, and language systems of the respective intelligences.

Assessing Interpersonal Intelligence

Interpersonal intelligence assessments ask students to demonstrate their knowledge and learning as part of a group or cooperative effort. The primary mode of this assessment is meaningful person-to-person relating and effective teamwork, including such things as reflective listening, trust of teammates, encouragement and support of others, division of labor, empathy, consensus, and transcending self-interest for the sake of the success of the team.

Interpersonal assessments require students to use verbal and nonverbal communication skills; sensitivity to others' moods, motives, and feelings; co-operation within a group ("positive interdependence"); discernment of another's underlying intentions and perspectives based on behavior; and the creation and maintenance of synergy (*synergy* comes from the Greek *syn ergos,* which means "a spontaneous working together"). Students must show their individual learning and knowledge as part of a group effort, by helping the group succeed, or by teaching others.

Guidelines for Creating Interpersonal Content Rubrics

Interpersonal intelligence assessments challenge students to demonstrate their understanding and grasp of curricular concepts as part of a collaborative effort. Your job is to look for conceptual mastery in and through various kinds of cooperative interactions with classmates, for example, working with partners, creating group projects, cooperative learning activities, and so on. You are assessing their interpersonal capacities, their skill and effectiveness to operate as part of a team. Use everything you know about evaluating cooperative learning groups to assist you. From the standpoint of evaluating their academic progress (or evaluating their learning) your main concern is with the cognitive process, or the unique way of knowing, represented by interpersonal intelligence. The knowing that occurs is seen in and through the process of human beings relating to and communicating with others, as well as in the very process of group or team dynamics themselves. It involves such things as listening to and understanding another's communication and being able to learn from another; being able to teach another person something; giving another person accurate and helpful feedback and receiving such feedback; and "piggybacking" ideas on other's ideas so that the ultimate learning is more than anyone could have achieved alone. The key is to learn to "read" and interpret these interpersonal representations for students' actual understanding of the material being assessed.

Sample Rubrics for Interpersonal Intelligence

 ## Cooperative Group Jigsaws

Performing an assessment or examination as a team with each member doing part of the exam then checking one another's work

INTELLIGENCE PERFORMANCE

Basic-Level Rubric

- Takes part in the cooperative group exactly as outlined by the teacher

Complex-Level Rubric

- Takes part in the cooperative group but goes beyond the initial guidelines

Higher-Order Rubric

- Takes full responsibility for the team, doing part as outlined but also assisting others

CONTENT UNDERSTANDING

Questions to Ask Myself

- Where do I feel I need to probe answers to make sure students have really understood, even though their answer is "correct"?
- Where do I need to discuss their answers because they are not quite on target, but I think they understand?
- Do I sense there are some students who genuinely understand the material but couldn't produce it working with a group?

Questions to Ask Students

- "Please expand on your answer and tell me why or how you know it is right." OR "This answer isn't quite right. As a team, can you fix it?"
- "As you look over your individual answers, are there any whose accuracy you question and want to discuss with your team?"
- "Do any of you feel you would like an individual conference to more fully explain your thinking and answers to me?"

▶ Explaining to or Teaching Another

Telling another person the answer to a question on an examination and explaining why the answer is accurate

INTELLIGENCE PERFORMANCE

Basic-Level Rubric

- Explanation is "the facts, ma'am; nothing but the facts" or "that's what the book says!"

Complex-Level Rubric

- Explanation includes why and how the information given is accurate or inaccurate

Higher-Order Rubric

- Explanation includes how the information or answer is applicable or transferable

CONTENT UNDERSTANDING

Questions to Ask Myself

- Where do I sense that a student knows and understands more than was in the explanation?
- Did I hear inaccurate explanations or teachings that need to be corrected?
- As they were explaining and teaching where did they show significant understanding beyond my expectations?

Questions to Ask Students

- "How did you arrive at the answer you explained and taught each other?"
- "This part of your explanation is not quite right. Can you work together to correct it?" OR "Can you find another pair or another person to help you?"
- "Please elaborate on or expand your answer a bit. I think you know and understand more than your answer reveals."

Think-Pair-Share

Telling answers to another who in turn tells another and so on around a cooperative group

INTELLIGENCE PERFORMANCE

Basic-Level Rubric

- Simply repeats the information exactly as it was communicated by previous partner

Complex-Level Rubric

- Elaborates on the information received from a partner and checks for understanding

Higher-Order Rubric

- Elaborates on the information received and enters into serious dialogue with partners

CONTENT UNDERSTANDING

Questions to Ask Myself

- Do I hear students helping and correcting one another before passing it on to another?
- Do I hear inaccurate information that needs to be corrected before it is passed?
- Are students entering into a genuine, sharing dialogue in which they probe one another's understanding?

Questions to Ask Students

- "I liked the way you worked to correct one another's answers. What told you that there may be a problem with a particular answer?"
- "Can you work further with your partner to improve this answer? It needs some work!"
- "What questions could you ask one another that would help you know if an answer is correct?"

▶ Round Robin

Performing a specified part of an examination, then passing it on for others to build on

INTELLIGENCE PERFORMANCE

Basic-Level Rubric
- Builds on another's work in a fairly linear, expected manner, simply adding more data or information

Complex-Level Rubric
- Builds on another's work by integrating own responses

Higher-Order Rubric
- Uses the work, thinking, and responses of others as a springboard to promote new levels of understanding for the group

CONTENT UNDERSTANDING

Questions to Ask Myself
- Where do I see one student discussing and correcting another's work before building on it?
- Where do I sense that, even though a "wrong" answer was produced, the student really understands the information?
- Where is the building on close but not quite on target, and I feel a comment from me would help the student be more accurate?

Questions to Ask Students
- "What you have built on is not quite accurate, but it's close. Can you work with the previous person and correct it?"
- "I know you understand this information even though your answer is incorrect. Can you talk to me about your understanding?"
- "How did you know if the answer you were building onto was correct?"

Giving and Receiving Feedback

Evaluating team members' responses to examination questions, then coaching one another to come up with better answers

INTELLIGENCE PERFORMANCE

Basic-Level Rubric

- Feedback and evaluation are based on whether or not the information exactly matches the information as it was originally given (that is, in the textbook or from you)

Complex-Level Rubric

- Feedback involves asking teammates to expand on and more fully explain initial responses and answers

Higher-Order Rubric

- Feedback involves genuine dialogue with teammates in which answers given are probed and examined for thorough understanding

CONTENT UNDERSTANDING

Questions to Ask Myself

- Where do I hear crystal clear evaluations and very effective coaching occurring, which tells me they really understand?
- Where do I need to intervene in the process because students are stuck or giving one another inaccurate information?
- Do I see some students who are having difficulty receiving the feedback from their partner so I need to intervene?

Questions to Ask Students

- "What do you remember from the studying we have been doing of this information?"
- "What can I do to help with your understanding of and listening to one another's feedback so that we learn as much as possible?"
- "Let's give clues as feedback. What clues (not answers) could you give that would help your partner more fully understand the information?"

▶ Interviews, Questionnaires, and People Searches

Getting answers from one another for questions on an examination and knowing if the answers are accurate

INTELLIGENCE PERFORMANCE

Basic-Level Rubric

- Evaluates an answer to a question based on how closely it resembles the form of the original information

Complex-Level Rubric

- Recognizes an accurate response to an examination question when someone has used own words to explain a concept

Higher-Order Rubric

- Identifies an accurate response by questioning to make sure that the one giving the response truly understands the answer

CONTENT UNDERSTANDING

Questions to Ask Myself

- Where do I see students questioning one another's responses to correct inaccuracies or to ensure accuracy or understanding?
- Where do I fear that some students are simply accepting all answers and not questioning if the answers are correct?
- Do I hear some students agreeing that an answer is correct when it is not? Do I need to intervene?

Questions to Ask Students

- "Are you sure that is the correct answer? Talk to me about it. How do you know it's correct?"
- "What made you ask the questions you did to check the accuracy of that response?"
- "What could you do to check the accuracy of that answer?"

Empathetic Processing

Demonstrating understanding of a partner's answer to a question and why the answer is correct or incorrect

INTELLIGENCE PERFORMANCE

Basic-Level Rubric

- Can accurately repeat an answer or response given by a partner, including why the person believes the answer is correct or not

Complex-Level Rubric

- Communicates an answer or response from a partner, including some of the partner's affective responses regarding its relative accuracy

Higher-Order Rubric

- Speaks wholly from the perspective of the partner, trying to justify, amend, or expand on the partner's responses

CONTENT UNDERSTANDING

Questions to Ask Myself

- Where do I see genuine concern that each partner understands, and in-depth conversation about the topic is occurring?
- Where do I see a student's understanding displayed through or embedded in dialogue over a partner's answer?
- Do I sense that some students are simply accepting another's response to make the partners feel good or because they are afraid to question?

Questions to Ask Students

- "Please tell me more about the conversation you have been having about the information. What led you to this discussion?"
- "How do you know if what your partner told you is right? What questions do you need to be asking yourself?"
- "I heard you saying x in response to your partner's answer. Why did you say that? What was the thinking behind your response?"

▶ Random Group Quizzes

Studying certain ideas as a team, then answering questions about the material as you randomly choose various group members

INTELLIGENCE PERFORMANCE

Basic-Level Rubric

- Answers questions by reproducing the facts, data, basic information exactly as the group discussed or studied it

Complex-Level Rubric

- Answers questions by accurately recalling the information but expressing it in own words

Higher-Order Rubric

- Summarizes and synthesizes what the group studied or discussed

CONTENT UNDERSTANDING

Questions to Ask Myself

- Where do I know they understand even though they didn't produce the correct answer?
- Where do I need to probe an answer to see if the student really understands or if it was a lucky guess?
- Where do I need to throw an individual's answer back to the group for further discussion before I accept it?

Questions to Ask Students

- "Can you answer the question (or explain a concept) if I ask the question a different way? I know you know this information."
- "Yes, that is the correct answer, but can you answer a couple of questions I have about your answer?"
- "I'm going to ask your group to discuss the answer you have given to the question: Is it correct? Why or why not? What would be a better answer?"

▶ # Assess Your Teammates

Making up authentic assessments for one another, administering the assessments, and checking the answers for understanding

INTELLIGENCE PERFORMANCE

Basic-Level Rubric

- The assessment looks only for basic facts, data, and recall of otherwise memorized information

Complex-Level Rubric

- The assessment looks for basic facts and an understanding of the relationships, dynamics, and processes involved with the facts

Higher-Order Rubric

- The assessment is concerned with integration, synthesis, transfer, and application of the facts, information, and concepts

CONTENT UNDERSTANDING

Questions to Ask Myself

- Where do I see genuine understanding of the concepts being assessed?
- Where are the assessments they have designed slightly (or greatly) not on target? Do I need to intervene?
- Where do I sense that a student understands a great deal more than is shown in the teammate's test?

Questions to Ask Students

- "Please explain your questions to me and the answers you are looking for. What would constitute a 'right' answer?"
- "If you had to give a full answer to a question you have created for another, what would you say?"
- "What questions do you wish you had been asked in order to more fully show your understanding?"

▶ Test, Coach, and Retest

Discussing the questions missed on a test and helping one another to understand the mistakes, then retaking the test

INTELLIGENCE PERFORMANCE

Basic-Level Rubric

- Returns to the book or notes to look for the "right" answers

Complex-Level Rubric

- Analyzes an incorrect answer to understand why or how it is incorrect and what a correct answer would look like

Higher-Order Rubric

- Evaluates any answer or response for how it could be correct or incorrect given certain variables (is open to several possible "right" answers)

CONTENT UNDERSTANDING

Questions to Ask Myself

- Where do I hear students' real understanding coming through in their coaching, even though they didn't represent it on the test itself?
- Do I see good coaching with inaccurate information? Do I need to intervene or reteach something?
- Where do I see understanding growing in and through the coaching process? Where are they not only correcting their mistakes but grasping implications of the correct or incorrect answers?

Questions to Ask Students

- "Please talk to me more about what you were telling your partner in the coaching process."
- "What questions about the material have been raised for you in the coaching process? Where are you not confident that you and your partner really understand?"
- "In the coaching process what are the key things you learned from and with your coach?"

Interpersonal Teacher Examples

ᴍ Government Exam

This example provided by Sharon Neifer demonstrates an ingenious use of interpersonal intelligence to assess various aspects of students' real understanding of several concepts of a government. This exam is an excellent example of the importance of in-context learning and the importance of seeing students apply knowledge to thoroughly assess their understanding as opposed to the simple recall of information. The evaluation criteria page allows students to know up front what is expected. In principle, all teams could score 100 points on the exam. The form that asks students to evaluate their teammates' contribution promotes a deeper awareness of interpersonal intelligence and the possibility of increasing skill.

The Activity

Students are asked to help a new country form a government. The leaders of the country need to write a constitution. They wonder if the people need something similar to the Bill of Rights. They also wonder if the government should be in control of everything for a while.

Students make a chart that shows the forms of government they know about, then decide what form of government this country should have. A direct or indirect democracy? Army rule? Perhaps the new country will need to have branches in its government. Perhaps it would be better off with localized government. Students make a case for or against having a bill of rights. They make a diagram that shows ways they would set up the government, then write a basic constitution.

The Assessment

The exam is evaluated primarily based on completeness of information, with a mark of excellent (10 points) given in categories that are complete and that have no mistakes, skilled (5 points) given for incomplete information with a few mistakes, and need help (0 points) for aspects that were not done and for more than four errors. Students are also asked to evaluate their teammates' effort, attitude, work completed, and goals met on a scale of 1 (inadequate) to 10 (excellent).

Total Quality Management Teams

The next example was submitted by Mary Porter. This lesson is a fine demonstration of a way to set up and orchestrate cooperative groups at the high school level; the tasks require a team and would be next to impossible to perform alone, resulting in what Roger and David Johnson have called "positive interdependence." In and through the very process of the activity, most capacities of interpersonal intelligence are called to the fore. There is a seamless weaving of the intelligence with the content; they are inseparable. The form that students fill out to evaluate their own and their team members' cooperative behavior, while not a rubric, gives students a sense of empowerment and ownership of the assessment. All schools of cooperative learning underscore the importance of the group processing piece as a way to help students become better at group work, or in the language of this book, at using their interpersonal intelligence.

The Activity

The objective of the activity is to establish class rules and consequences. In a five-minute brainstorm session, students list eight to ten rules they feel the classroom needs and why each rule is important. They place asterisks beside the top five and write each rule on a separate sheet of paper, then put up each rule around the room, grouping rules with similar rules from other teams. The whole class looks at the rule groupings. Each team presents their rules and justifies them. The class creates a bar graph of all the rules and decides on the top five rules. They post the five rules around the room, then list the possible consequences for breaking each rule on individual sheets of paper. They post the lists beside the rules. The class discusses the consequences and chooses a consequence that it will enforce for each broken rule.

The Assessment

Students rate criteria from 1 to 5 with 1 being low; 2, adequate; 3, average; 4, above average; and 5, excellent. The criteria include their own participation in brainstorming and consensus building, their ability to get along with team members and to allow others to express their ideas, and their demonstration of responsibility. They then evaluate their team as a whole on the same criteria. Finally, they state ways they think they could improve the team process and consensus building.

Helping Hands

The next example comes from Jennifer Colasanti. The lesson starts with asking elementary students to think of things they can do individually to be good friends, then moves to incorporating and honoring the contributions of the individuals. The very simple rubric is based on the teams' progressing precisely in this way. What a great way to access the capacities of interpersonal intelligence.

The Activity

The objective of this lesson is to help students learn ways to be better friends. Students trace around their hands and cut the tracings out. They write on their cutouts things they can do to "lend a hand" and be good friends to others, then place the cutouts on the bulletin board, overlapping them slightly. In addition to the interpersonal intelligence, students use verbal-linguistic, visual-spatial, and intrapersonal intelligences. Finally, in groups of four, students develop simple skits to act out the things they chose to write on their cutouts.

The Assessment

Groups receive 1 point for each child whose ideas they incorporate, up to 4 points. 1 bonus point is given if they demonstrate why the actions are important.

Extended Postcard

The following example is from the Eureka Project. It is the first part of the intrapersonal T-shirt activity. I include them because they clearly illustrate something I mention in the introduction to the personal intelligence rubrics; namely, the personal intelligences are, in some ways, two sides of a single coin. Both lessons and assessment begin with the individual and move to the group. The intrapersonal work, for the most part, involves various introspective, self-reflective exercises. The interpersonal work involves sharing individual work as well as listening to and appreciating others' work. The main focus of these lessons is to help students get to know their inter- and intrapersonal intelligences. But these examples also extend into the traditional academic areas relatively easily.

The Activity

Individual students fill out postcards that include one of the following in each corner: a favorite TV program, a place they would like to visit, something they are good at, and something they would like to accomplish. The class forms a circle. Students share the information of the first corner with the students beside them. They paraphrase what each says. Each finds another partner with whom to share corner 2 and paraphrase what the partner says. They continue for the remaining points. Note that this activity can be done in social groups as well as in school. If the group has advanced social skills, partners can become groups of four, then eight. Your students can create a "Who's Who in the Classroom" booklet or a class HyperCard, survey and graph, or other visual representation. Primary grades may limit activity to the community circle. In addition to the interpersonal intelligence, students use verbal-linguistic and intrapersonal intelligences. They develop cooperative circle as well as active listening skills.

The Assessment

Students' cooperative group skills are assessed as undeveloped if the students work alone, even in the group, and if their social skills are undeveloped. Group skills are assessed as developing if students will participate in the groups and help develop models or visual aids. The skills are assessed as highly developed if students suggest collaboration, promote cohesiveness, and act as facilitators for groups. Students' communication skills are assessed as undeveloped if students listen actively to others and contribute to the group discussion only occasionally. Communication skills are assessed as developing if students listen actively and contribute their ideas and opinions, and if they use metacognition to develop their social skills. Finally the skills are highly developed if the students communicate with others verbally and nonverbally, are empathetic to diverse opinions, and display an ability to handle conflicts.

Assessing Intrapersonal Intelligence

Intrapersonal intelligence assessments (introspective assessments) ask students to demonstrate their knowledge and learning through expression of what they feel about the material and how it may have informed or changed their own understanding, personal philosophy, beliefs, and values.

Intrapersonal assessments require students to use concentration; mindfulness (attention to the myriad details of life or "stop and smell the roses"); metacognitive processing (thinking about and analyzing own patterns of thinking); awareness and expression of various feelings; transpersonal sense of the self ("no one is an island"); and higher-order thinking and reasoning (such as Bloom's taxonomy). Students must show their knowledge of a subject in and through introspection about the topics using such things as reflective writing and speaking, symbolic representations of meanings and understandings, or applications of ideas beyond the classroom.

Guidelines for Creating Intrapersonal Content Rubrics

Intrapersonal intelligence assessments challenge students to demonstrate their understanding and grasp of curricular concepts by going inside, so to speak, and reflecting on the personal meanings of what one is studying. Your job is to help students feel comfortable delving into the "inner world of the self" and to develop and value their introspective or self-reflective capabilities. You must look for their conceptual mastery in and through their thoughts, feelings, questions, inner wrestlings, and so on that surface as they are involved in using the assessment instruments. You will examine such inner products as reflections on what students find personally interesting, questions the material has raised about who they are, questions of life's meaning, personal goals, ways they think they can use the information, affective connections (or lack thereof), ability to transfer the learning to other subjects and beyond the school setting, their metacognitive behavior, and so on. As mentioned earlier, this intelligence is the most private of the intelligences; therefore, using intrapersonal intelligence to assess is somewhat like finding ways to eavesdrop on the conversations students have with themselves! Each instrument is designed to lead students into introspection and provide you with a way to catch them reflecting, that is, to notice *on what and about what* they are reflecting. The key is to learn to "read" and interpret these intrapersonal representations for students' actual understanding of the material being assessed.

Sample Rubrics for Intrapersonal Intelligence

▶ Autobiographical Reporting

Writing a report or speaking into a recorder on ways that a concept or idea from a lesson has informed or had an impact on self-understanding

INTELLIGENCE PERFORMANCE

Basic-Level Rubric

- Sees very few connections or only surface or obvious implications

Complex-Level Rubric

- Goes beyond the obvious and expected implications to articulate several new learnings, insights, discoveries, or reflections

Higher-Order Rubric

- Transforms the original information or concept into a profound articulation of self-discovery and even reevaluates identity

CONTENT UNDERSTANDING

Questions to Ask Myself

- What in the report surprises me with its reflection of understanding or interest in this topic?
- What do I see in the report that I really don't understand or find contradictory?
- Where do I sense the student somehow missed the point and I need to discuss with her?

Questions to Ask Students

- "Please tell me more about this part of your autobiographical report."
- "I don't understand how you arrived at these conclusions in your report. Please help me understand."
- "Let's revisit the information before the autobiography. How could you adjust the autobiography to more accurately reflect this?"

▶ Personal Application Scenarios

Telling ways that one could apply or use certain information or
concepts in the task of daily living beyond school

INTELLIGENCE PERFORMANCE

Basic-Level Rubric

- Scenario articulates a very linear, one-on-one, expected, obvious
  application

Complex-Level Rubric

- Statement of several not obvious applications that were derived
  through cross-lateral thinking about other subject areas and
  disciplines

Higher-Order Rubric

- Scenario shows thorough assimilation, integration, or transference
  of the concepts so they are part of a repertoire for living beyond
  formal education

CONTENT UNDERSTANDING

Questions to Ask Myself

- Where do I see applications that make me question if the student
  has really understood the concepts?
- What applications delight me because of the cleverness that also
  demonstrates deep understanding?
- Where do I sense that a student knows more than the scenario
  expresses?

Questions to Ask Students

- "I think you know more than you expressed in your scenario. What
  would help you tell me about it?"
- "I was fascinated with how you arrived at this way to apply the
  material. Can you tell me how you did it?"
- "How did you arrive at this application from these concepts?"

▶ # Metacognitive Surveys and Questionnaires

Relating how one approached particular problems and evaluating the strategies employed

INTELLIGENCE PERFORMANCE

Basic-Level Rubric

- Accurate restatement of the textbook steps for getting the right answer (little or no understanding of why these steps are taken)

Complex-Level Rubric

- Talks about intermediate steps and thinking employed in between the textbook steps (understands why the steps are taken)

Higher-Order Rubric

- More interested in the problem-solving process than in getting the so-called right answer (very aware of own thinking processes)

CONTENT UNDERSTANDING

Questions to Ask Myself

- What totally baffles me about how a student came up with a certain answer or conclusion?
- Where do I see a student who is fascinated more with the process than the facts, figures, and data?
- Where do I see a student who is aware of and using the correct process but still coming up with inaccurate answers or conclusions?

Questions to Ask My Students

- "I'm confused with how you came up with that answer. Can you take me back through your thought process?"
- "This answer is not quite right. Can you find your own mistakes?"
- "You have a great understanding of the process. Now can you apply it to the factual information of the topic?"

Higher-Order Questions and Answers

Recalling facts, then moving to understanding process, to applying, synthesizing, and integrating various dimensions of what has been studied

INTELLIGENCE PERFORMANCE

Basic-Level Rubric

- Accurately recalls and reproduces the basic facts, figures, and data

Complex-Level Rubric

- Exhibits a grasp of relationships, dynamics, connections, and processes among various facts, figures, and data

Higher-Order Rubric

- Demonstrates an understanding of how to use, apply, integrate, and synthesize the facts, figures, and data

CONTENT UNDERSTANDING

Questions to Ask Myself

- What leads me to feel that a student is stuck in the facts, not really understanding what they mean?
- Do I see a student who has moved to higher-order thinking but really isn't working with accurate information?
- Where am I seeing "thought-fullness" that is beyond anything I expect from a student, so I want to talk?

Questions to Ask My Students

- "You got the right answers. Now can you explain to me what the answers mean?"
- "I'm fascinated by your work here. Can you tell me how you are thinking about this material?"
- "What you have done here is very clever and creative. Are you sure that you really understand the related factual information?"

► Concentration Tests

Choosing a focus or foci from a list to demonstrate understanding and knowledge

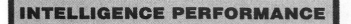

INTELLIGENCE PERFORMANCE

Basic-Level Rubric

- Chooses a very narrow focus and includes few or only minor details

Complex-Level Rubric

- Chooses several foci and presents many relevant details while maintaining the foci

Higher-Order Rubric

- Presents a broad focus that encompasses a full range of details related to the subject

CONTENT UNDERSTANDING

Questions to Ask Myself

- Where did a student begin with a clear focus but seem to lose it as the work progressed, so I need to help refocus?
- What leads me to believe that a student knows and understands the material but chose too narrow a focus and thus was unable to show true learning?
- Where am I amazed by the breadth and depth of what a student was able to demonstrate?

Questions to Ask Myself

- "I understand your initial focus. Please explain how *x* relates to that focus."
- "Please explain to me what you think the focus you chose means and what's involved in it."
- "What other foci from the options might have been better choices to help you demonstrate your understanding?"

▶ Feeling Diaries and Logs

Writing, speaking, and drawing about personal feelings or emotional responses to various subjects

INTELLIGENCE PERFORMANCE

Basic-Level Rubric
- Articulates surface, to-be-expected feelings or emotions that show basic personal connections

Complex-Level Rubric
- Expresses several levels of emotional response that indicate an understanding of deeper human motifs

Higher-Order Rubric
- Expresses being deeply touched or moved in fairly complex ways that show new aspects of the self have been opened

CONTENT UNDERSTANDING

Questions to Ask Myself
- What feelings about the material really catch me off guard so I need to talk with the student?
- Where do I sense a lot more going on with a student and this topic because of the emotional response?
- Which feelings expressed do I not understand or find confusing?

Questions to Ask Students
- "I'm really struck by the feelings you expressed. Can you tell me more about what's behind them?"
- "Can you tell me more about what in this material evoked these feelings you have expressed?"
- "How could you express these feelings in other ways (for example, color, symbols, music)?"

▶ # Personal Projection

Expressing "If I were . . . I would . . . " in relation to persons, characters, situations or concepts

INTELLIGENCE PERFORMANCE

Basic-Level Rubric

- Straight-line, linear, one-on-one projection that basically remains within the subject area

Complex-Level Rubric

- Nonlinear thinking about the information so the projection makes some interesting, creative leaps beyond the subject area

Higher-Order Rubric

- Thorough assimilation of the persons, situations, and concepts so that the projection is made from the perspective of being inside the information

CONTENT UNDERSTANDING

Questions to Ask Myself

- Where do the projections tell me the student really does not understand the material?
- Which projections demonstrate a deep identification with the material so I need to explore further?
- Where did I feel that the student was "one with the material"?

Questions to Ask My Students

- "I'm not sure how this part of your projection fits in. Can you help me understand your thinking?"
- "You seem to really be inside this material. Can you tell me how this happened?"
- "Why did you decide to do your projection on this aspect of the material as opposed to other possibilities?"

▶ # Self-Identification Reporting

Telling about personal likes and dislikes, and persons or situations with which identified

INTELLIGENCE PERFORMANCE

Basic-Level Rubric

- Identifies with the obvious, surface aspects of the subject, topic, or concepts

Complex-Level Rubric

- Sees a number of creative or surprising connections between the concepts and own life

Higher-Order Rubric

- Expresses multiple levels of analogical self-understanding in and through the report

CONTENT UNDERSTANDING

Questions to Ask Myself

- Where does a student's self-identification show more understanding than what is expressed?
- Where am I genuinely confused by the identification because it doesn't seem to fit the material?
- Where do I sense a student wants to know more or explore the concepts at hand more fully?

Questions to Ask My Students

- "You seem to really like this material. What else would you like to do that is related to this topic?"
- "I'm confused by your identification report. Can you explain how x, y, and z fit in with the material?"
- "Do you have more that you want to communicate to show me what you've learned?"

▶ # Personal History Correlation

Finding correlative patterns between own life and subjects being studied

INTELLIGENCE PERFORMANCE

Basic-Level Rubric

- Sensing only obvious correlations between own life and the information (Revolutionary War = "I rebel when others tell me what to do without my input")

Complex-Level Rubric

- Noticing the obvious connections but also grasping potential learning discoveries and advice for self (Revolutionary War = "Many struggles of the colonists are similar to struggles in my life.")

Higher-Order Rubric

- Expressing ways own life has been deeply informed, moved, and altered by the information; learning is inseparable from the learner (Revolutionary War = "In my life the Declaration of Independence is . . . " or "My Boston Tea Party was . . . "

CONTENT UNDERSTANDING

Questions to Ask Myself

- What correlations in a student's work surprise me because he made connections I didn't anticipate?
- What correlations make me seriously question if the student understands the material?
- What could I do to help the student see more correlations where there are few or where they seem "off the wall"?

Questions to Ask My Students

- "If you had to think of at least three more correlations between your life and this material, what would they be?"
- "I don't understand this correlation. Please help me understand your thinking."
- "How did you arrive at the correlations you have seen?"

Personal Priorities, Values, and Goals

Reporting how a subject affected one's priorities, values, and goals

INTELLIGENCE PERFORMANCE

Basic-Level Rubric

- Accurately reports the basic facts but sees little or no impact on self

Complex-Level Rubric

- Makes number of connections to the self via feelings, questions raised, things that are personally interesting, and so on

Higher-Order Rubric

- Expresses many potential shifts in values, priorities, self-understandings, personal philosophy, and so on

CONTENT UNDERSTANDING

Questions to Ask Myself

- Where has a student been deeply impacted by the material?
- Where does a student seem to have somehow missed the point by not seeing any personal relevance?
- Where do I feel I need to ask more questions about the impact of the material?

Questions to Ask My Students

- "Can you tell me more about the impact of this material on you? Why do you think it affected you so strongly?"
- "Why do you feel that this material has no meaning or relevance for you?"
- "As you think about this material, what are all of the possible implications you can think of?"

Intrapersonal Teacher Examples

Unique Individuals

The next example comes from Jennifer Colasanti. The lesson and assessment demonstrate an ingenious use of intrapersonal intelligence for elementary children. The lesson shows a way to trigger introspection in young children, which as I mentioned earlier, is key to working effectively with the intrapersonal intelligence. The rubric is designed to help students make these inner self-knowings objective.

The Activity

The objective of this activity is to help students become aware of themselves as unique individuals. The class discusses unique qualities that make us individuals. Children respond to the following questions and statements:

- Name something you do well.
- Tell about something that is very important to you.
- Tell about your favorite memory.
- What is your favorite thing?
- Name something you do by yourself.
- What makes you laugh?
- Tell about the best time of your day.

They then use pictures and magazine cutouts, personal articles, and so on, to construct personal collages that depict the things that make them unique. Students present their collages to the class and give oral presentations. In addition to the intrapersonal intelligences, students use verbal-linguistic, visual-spatial, and interpersonal intelligences.

The Assessment

The collages are assessed, with 1 point being given for a basic collage that lacks adequate reflection and explanation, 2 points for a concise collage that has adequate reflection and explanation, and 3 points for an elaborate collage that shows thoughtful reflection and elaboration.

Intrapersonal T-Shirt

The following example is a companion activity to the extended postcard activity in the interpersonal section. See comments page 164.

The Activity

Students bring in white or light-colored T-shirts. They preplan T-shirts on newsprint cut to their sizes and shapes. They decorate the newsprint T-shirt by placing their names in the center, graffiti style. They each write a positive adjective about themselves under their name. They draw two things they like to do in their spare time on one sleeve, and two ways they learn best on the other sleeve. In one bottom corner, students each draw a picture of themselves as they think they will look in ten years, and in the other bottom corner, a picture of a goal to complete by the next year. Finally, they create a symbol that represents them, such as a flower with a smiling face or a car, at the top. They decorate the rest of the T-shirt with doodles and sketches. They use fabric markers to copy the designs onto their shirts and share the shirts with the class, explaining each part. For younger students, substitute items they identify with. In addition to the intrapersonal intelligence, students use visual-spatial and verbal-linguistic intelligences. They learn how to encourage others and take turns, and learn such thinking skills as attributing, perceiving, and metacognition.

The Assessment

Students' ability to self-direct is assessed as undeveloped if they are dependent on others for making their decisions or must have goals set for them. This ability is assessed as developing if students need guidance to see possibilities beyond the obvious, and highly developed if students naturally set short- and long-term goals based on situations. Students' ability to reflect is assessed as undeveloped if they do not have a personal reflection event, as developing if they reflect when directed to do so, and as highly developed if they reflect and act on reflections and explore thoughts, feelings, and moods.

7
Eight-in-One Examples
*Bringing It All Together*_____

This last section is devoted to examples that incorporate all the intelligences. I was not anticipating that teachers would send me so many examples that demonstrate how to use all or most of the intelligences in a given assessment process. I find these examples particularly exciting and provocative because they show that it is indeed possible to give equal weight to all the intelligences and to value each way of knowing without having to say one is somehow better or more important than another.

Several things make these multiple intelligence approaches very interesting:

1. A most compelling piece of contemporary research indicates that **the more you stir up neurological processes, the greater the learning that occurs.** In other words, the more levels of the brain-mind-body system on which we know something, the more genuinely we know it. So if you can write it, talk about it, sing it, dance it, draw and paint it, sculpt it, talk with someone else about it, reflect on it, and logically analyze it, the more deeply you understand it. The eight-in-one approach moves knowing beyond just head knowledge.

2. Multimodal assessments give us a way to **catalyze a lot more student interest** in the material. William Glasser points out that the number one problem we face in public education in the Western world is that a majority of students have no desire whatsoever to be in school. I think an approach to teaching, learning, and assessment that engages all levels of a student's *human being* cannot help but create an *intrinsic motivation* to learn.

3. This approach gives teachers a means par excellence to pursue our main objective as educators, namely, to **go for the deep assessment— the assessment of students' genuine understanding of the curriculum.** There are a number of other benefits to teachers, including keeping things interesting for us; it helps keep us on our toes regarding our students' creativity, and it helps us maintain our own creative edge.

4. If we **train parents in MI**, there is probably nothing we can do that will bring about a greater change in their involvement in their child's education. Through many parent workshops, I have learned that parents know their children are smart, but not necessarily in the way school values. Inject MI into the formula, and suddenly, we have a way to help parents learn how to use their children's unique way of knowing to be successful. In my experience, this success is all the convincing most parents need. A secondary benefit is that MI can often give parents a new understanding of and appreciation for their child's unique qualities.

5. A multimodal approach provides one of the best ways for administrators to **maintain high standards in their schools or districts**. Far from lowering standards, an MI approach to curriculum development, instruction, and assessment can very quickly move the entire educational enterprise to the upper levels of Bloom's famous taxonomy, albeit into intelligence-specific higher-order levels. Unfortunately, currently no standardized test that really values and assesses this kind of thorough knowing exists. Nevertheless, I can almost certainly guarantee that MI will not hurt students' performance on current standardized tests, and MI approaches to instruction and assessment give us the best shot at drastically improving scores on these tests.

The key to understanding the lessons and assessments that follow is remembering that each requires students to demonstrate their understanding using all or most of the intelligences through a single assessment instrument.

■ English Research Project

This example comes from Karen Rafacz. It is a fine demonstration of a way to use various intelligences to enhance a traditional high school research project. While it is not strictly an eight-in-one example, I include it here because it gives students options to use all the intelligences in the final project. One thing I especially like about this example is that it gives very clear guidelines for the research itself, then gives students many options for presenting their research. They do the research, then must do something with it! It also gives them opportunities to work with partners. The rubrics are focused on their final performance.

The Activity

Alone or with partners, students complete a research project on a famous person who has made a worthwhile contribution to the world. Individually, they must complete at least three bibliography cards (one for each source), one or more note cards for each source, a final outline that covers all the information, and a bibliography page that lists all their sources. Students then choose the final project from a list or come up with their own with teacher approval. The project must demonstrate all the information about their subject. Some of the projects are for single work (S), others are for pairs (P), and others can be either (S/P).

> *Traditional research report (S)*
>
> *Front page news story with a headline (S/P)*
>
> *Persuasive letter to the editor asking to name a new school after your subject (S/P)*
>
> *Poem (S/P)*
>
> *Labeled map that shows the location of major events in subject's life (S/P)*
>
> *Time line that shows major events in subject's life (S/P)*
>
> *Poster (S/P)*
>
> *Song (record it) (S/P)*
>
> *Talk-show interview (P)*
>
> *Skit (P)*

The Assessment

Students' work is evaluated in four categories.

Level 4

- Match to Research: Contains all information on note cards and in outline
- Content: Covers all three subtopics; contains more than enough information on each
- Presentation Clarity: Information is clear and easy to follow; stated in own words; leaves no questions

- Production: Professional; obvious time spent on preparing presentation; clean and neat; ready for the world to see or hear

Level 3

- Match to Research: Contains most information on note cards and in outline
- Content: Covers all three subtopics; includes minimum information on each
- Presentation Clarity: Most information clearly given and stated in own words; may leave a few questions
- Production: Semi-professional; could be more polished but definitely a good job; some rough edges; tiny bit of polish and it's ready for the big time

Level 2

- Match to Research: Contains some information found in note cards and on outline
- Content: Covers at least two subtopics; includes minimum information
- Presentation Clarity: Minimal; much not stated in own words; many questions
- Production: Pro-Am; almost ready for the big leagues but needs work in appearance or structure

Level 1

- Match to Research: Contains little of the information found in note cards and on outline
- Content: Covers only one subtopic; information is scant throughout
- Presentation Clarity: Very difficult to follow and understand; not stated in own words; leaves questions
- Production: Amateur; minimal project completed but needs improvement in many aspects

---

■ Character Traits in "Jack and the Beanstalk"

This example is from Ann Krone. It gives students choices of ways to demonstrate their understanding of Jack's character traits. The scoring criteria, while not a rubric, clearly value responses from all intelligences; students are assessed using the same criteria regardless of the project they choose.

The Activity

Students identify the character traits of Jack in "Jack and the Beanstalk." They read through several descriptions of activities, then select one and respond completely. The examples used here are by students.

- Verbal-linguistic (word smart). Pretend you are Jack and write an entry in his diary. Be sure to reveal a character trait. Student example: "Today I was determined to make my mother proud of me. After waking up, I looked out my window to see the huge beanstalk. Being a *curious* boy, I decided to climb the beanstalk to see what was at the top. Wow! A giant's castle!"

- Logical-mathematical (logic and number smart). Select two of Jack's character traits and show evidence of each trait in a graphic organizer. Student example is in graphic organizer, with evidence "Truly believed that the beans were magic" indicating first trait "*Has faith in others*," and evidence "Took all the giant's treasures" indicating second trait, "*greedy*."

- Visual-spatial (picture smart). Draw a picture that illustrates a situation that exists because of one of Jack's character traits. Student example: Student drew picture of Jack holding money bags, harp, and goose to show "*greedy*."

- Bodily-kinesthetic (body smart). Create a play that has Jack, his mother, and the giant (you play all three parts). Choose one of Jack's character traits and demonstrate it in your play. Student example: "Mother: Jack, you are so *foolish*! You traded a cow for worthless beans. I'm throwing them away!" "Jack: Wow! A beanstalk has grown outside my window. I *love adventure*. I think I'll climb it." "Giant: Fee, fi, fo, fum, I smell the blood of an Englishman. I am *mean* and destroy anyone who gets in my way. I'll eat this boy."

- Musical-rhythmic (sound smart). Change the words of a familiar song to illustrate one of Jack's character traits.

    Steal, steal, steal the gold—
    Take it down the beanstalk.
    Jack's a greedy little boy
    Hides it in a sock.

    Steal, steal, steal the harp
    Take it down the beanstalk.
    Jack's a greedy little boy
    Buys some bonds and stock.

- Interpersonal (people smart). With a partner, create a new ending to the story that results because of one of Jack's character traits. Student example: "After Jack took the giant's gold, harp, and golden eggs, he had a change of heart and decided to talk to the giant about how they could work together to help the unfortunate people on Earth."

- Intrapersonal (self smart). Select one of Jack's character traits and complete the following sentence starter: "If I were Jack, I would . . . " Explain why you would behave in a certain way or say something and give an example. Student example: "If I were Jack, I would be an obedient son and take the cow to market. I wouldn't be *disobedient* like Jack was."

The Assessment

Students must accurately identify a trait. For example, they would identify a character who blows down someone's house as "mean." They must also provide evidence that supports their choices. For example, "John interrupted Jane three times, which proves he is rude."

■ Presentation Rubric

There is no activity with this rubric. The assessment from Ann Krone is a challenging, involved rubric by which any student project or presentation can be judged. It presupposes students' use of all the intelligences. It can be easily adapted to any conceivable curriculum.

The Assessment

1: Not There Yet

- Volume control: Hard to hear you
- Eye contact with audience: Very little, if any
- Visual aids: Did not use
- Attentive to topic: Not clear; very blurry
- Assessment of audience: Used skinny questions
- Use of Resources: Hearsay and encyclopedia

2: On Your Way

- Volume control: Heard you, but hard to understand you
- Eye contact with audience: Sometimes; occasionally looked
- Visual aids: Ineffective use that was not helpful
- Attentive to topic: Knew what you meant most of the time; a little blurry
- Assessment of audience: Used medium questions
- Use of Resources: Encyclopedia and another resource

3: It's a Hit!

- Volume control: Heard and understood most of the time
- Eye contact with audience: Looked at audience, but uncomfortably
- Visual aids: Used to improve presentation
- Attentive to topic: Knew what you meant; clearly understood
- Assessment of audience: Used fat questions
- Use of Resources: Encyclopedia and two other resources

4: Number 1 on the Charts

- Volume control: Easy to hear and understand you
- Eye contact with audience: Included everyone; relaxed and comfortable
- Visual aids: Imaginative and useful
- Attentive to topic: Enlightening; focused on topic to make understanding clear
- Assessment of audience: WOW! Reflected intense critical thinking
- Use of Resources: Encyclopedia and at least three different types of resources

■ Contemporary Art History Final

I include the following three examples from Ann Krone because they are MI assessment activities being used in higher education. The tasks are laid out clearly and need no further explanation. The exam has assessment criteria, although they are not a rubric.

The Activity

- Create a game and game board that uses the major art styles of the twentieth century as its theme.
- Write a personal reflection about all the major styles.
- Write a poem about the evolution of art through the twentieth century.
- Create a flip book that animates an object that moves through the major styles.
- Write a monologue for a paintbrush that gets moved from style to style and artist to artist.
- Create cause-and-effect diagrams that link historic events with events in art.

The Assessment

- Portrays a major event for the period
- Portrays major artists for the period
- Interprets the significance of the historical period
- Communicates the flavor or mood of the period
- Portrays social, political, or religious features of the period
- Relates accurate information regarding all the above

■ Aesthetic and "Anaesthetic"

See comments under the previous example, Contemporary Art History Final. These activities do not include assessments.

The Activities

- Verbal-linguistic: Write a description of a common object, such as a telephone. Describe it aesthetically in one paragraph and "anaesthetically" in another. Write several paragraphs in which you describe the difference between an aesthetic experience and an "anaesthetic" experience.
- Logical-mathematical: Create an if . . . then statement about your understanding of aesthetic and "anaesthetic." Draw a Venn diagram to compare the qualities of an aesthetic and an "anaesthetic" experience.
- Visual-spatial: Create a collage that shows the same object in the two different perspectives that merge in the center. Create a drawing or sculpture that expresses the difference between aesthetic and "anaesthetic."
- Musical-rhythmic: Create a musical composition on the instrument of your choice that expresses the difference between aesthetic and "anaesthetic." Rewrite the words of a familiar song such as "Row, Row, Row Your Boat" so that it describes the differences between aesthetic and "anaesthetic."
- Bodily-kinesthetic: Create a dance that shows the difference between aesthetic and "anaesthetic" and perform it for your class. Mime the differences between aesthetic and "anaesthetic."
- Interpersonal: With a partner, create a dialogue between two people who experience the same event (skiing, eating spinach, watching a movie); one has an aesthetic experience and the other, an "anaesthetic" experience.

- Intrapersonal: Write about an activity that you have experienced in both ways, anaesthetically and aesthetically. Write your personal feelings about the two experiences. Reflect about a time when you had an aesthetic experience and the person you were with had an anaesthetic experience. What did you do? What about the times when the roles were reversed? What did you do to change your attitude?

■ Study of Henry Moore

See comments under previous activity, Contemporary Art History Final. This example does not include an assessment.

The Activities

- Verbal-linguistic: Write a description of a Henry Moore sculpture; read a critique of Henry Moore's art; write a poem about Henry Moore's sculpture.
- Bodily-kinesthetic: Imagine that another person in the class is a lump of clay and fashion them into a Henry Moore sculpture; as an individual, act out the metamorphosis of a Moore sculpture from the raw material to the finished work.
- Logical-mathematical: Complete one of these statements "If Henry Moore's subject were flowers instead of women, then his art would change by . . . "; "If Henry Moore's sculpture were turned into a code, it would be . . . "
- Visual-spatial: Create a work of art that expresses the same theme as one of Henry Moore's sculptures; walk around a Henry Moore sculpture and, as you walk, draw a continuous line that shows what you see.
- Interpersonal: Re-create one of Henry Moore's sculptures with some of your classmates; as a group, create a semantic web about the characteristics and qualities of Henry Moore's sculpture.
- Intrapersonal: Draw a Henry Moore sculpture, then write your feelings about the various aspects of the sculpture inside the part of the drawing that corresponds to the part you are writing about; Select a Henry Moore sculpture that has a hole in it. Study the meaning of the hole in the sculpture and write your ideas inside a hole you draw.

■ "Dear Parents . . . "

The next example comes from Becky Supercinski. I include this letter and rubric because the effort to help parents understand MI and value students' work is a vital aspect of long-term success and acceptance of the theory of MI in schools. The assessment is a traditional assessment, based on a point system and generalized criteria.

The Activity

Parents are sent a letter that states the topic, "The Brain and Learning Styles." The letter briefly describes the assignment, to report on a chosen genius in one of the intelligences, and to create a presentation other than a written report on the choice. Examples include pretending to be the genius, dramatizing an important event in the life of the genius, and doing a mock interview. Students are asked to use at least four sources, with at least one being from the Internet, and to display their findings on a science-fair-type backboard. The parents are invited to the open house at which students will give their presentations.

The Assessment

Evidence of research including learning styles and analysis can earn the student a maximum 40 points; creativity of presentation, 30 points; use of the Internet, 20 points; and organization and display, 10 points.

■ Florida City Report

This example is from Jennifer Colasanti. The written and oral reports occur after students have done a fairly extensive research project. Although the final product is virtually all verbal-linguistic, students must include at least one item from each intelligence in their report. The assignment allows students to choose from a variety of presentations. This example does not include an assessment.

The Activity

Students are asked to report on a Florida city other than Miami. They look up reference materials about the city, write to the city's Chamber of Commerce, and access the Internet. They write and give an oral report that must include at least one of the following:

1. Verbal-linguistic: poem, descriptive paragraph, short story, written advertisement
2. Logical-mathematical: graph that shows size and population of city in comparison to Miami, word problem that uses some facts about the city, chart that shows the important industries, code and locations in the city for others to find

3. Visual-spatial: draw, paint, design, sculpt, cut and paste a map of the city

4. Bodily-kinesthetic: a role-play of a visit to a favorite point of interest, mime of how it feels to visit favorite point of interest, skit of pioneer deciding whether to settle in city

5. Musical-rhythmic: song about city using familiar tune, rap, found song that represents city

6. Interpersonal: game that requires two or more people to answer questions about city, activity that requires two or more people to show knowledge of city, group project to teach about city

7. Intrapersonal: paragraph about feelings toward city, location, and points of interest; paragraph that tells reasons you chose your city

■ Book Projects

The next example comes from Sharon Neifer. Sharon uses this approach instead of book reports. The project is a supreme example of how the instruction and assessment processes are two sides of a single coin. There is no separation between the learning activities and the assessment; students would, as they are creating their projects, assess their own and one another's work. The summary gives the teacher a wonderful screen for evaluating the finished products and for entering into dialogue with students about their work. An excellent way to use these rubrics would be to have students first score their individual book projects, then convince you that their scores are justified. Such an approach would offer countless opportunities to deepen students' understanding of the content of their projects and what is involved in producing a written product of quality.

The Activity

I have presented three projects in one; usually only three options are offered in each category. Students choose one item from each category for a total of four products.

1. Writing

- Write a continuation of this story.
- Write a fan letter to your favorite character. Explain why you are a fan.
- Change the ending of the story. Be sure to support your ending with facts.
- Rewrite a scene from your book, putting your characters in a different setting.
- Have one character write a letter to you that describes the main idea of the story.

- Write a poem that describes either a character or the setting of the story.
- Compare and contrast two characters.
- Write an advertisement for this book.

2. Research Skills

- Find out some factual information about the time setting of this book.
- In what part of the world does this story take place? Draw a map to show the location.
- Research the climate that you would find if you were a character in the book. Do an oral report on the climate.
- Research the setting of the book. Where in the world did it take place? How is it different or the same as today?
- Explain how the story would have changed if it had taken place in a different time.
- Describe the fashions the characters would wear.
- Make a collection of travel brochures and postcards to illustrate the settings of this book.
- Describe the setting of this book and compare it to the same place in 1776.
- Conduct a quiz show and use the information about the setting of the book.

3. Critical Analysis

- Evaluate the main character. What were the strengths? What were the weaknesses?
- Compare the beginning and ending of the story. How has the main character changed. What happened to create this change? Is it a good change? Explain.
- List the main characters. Explain their relationships throughout the book.
- Evaluate the main character. How would that character fit into today's society? Explain your answer.
- Describe your main characters. Who is the most cooperative? Who has the most empathy for others? Who has the fewest interpersonal conflicts?
- From the main characters, who would make a good best friend? Explain why.
- Prepare a board game using information from the book.
- Compose a song about a character or event in the book.
- Develop a crossword puzzle based on the book.

4. Expressive Arts

- Make a tabletop display that shows a scene from the book.
- Draw a mural that shows the scenes you feel are most important.
- Write a skit or play based on one part of the book. Cast classmates in the roles and present it to the class.
- Make a song or select a song that would go along with the mood or the time and place of your book.
- Draw or find pictures to show what you think the setting of the book looks like. Include some of the main characters in your picture.
- Design a game that would go with this book.
- Construct an advertising poster to promote your book.
- Paint a poster of a story scene.
- Use a comic strip format to depict episodes in the book.

The Assessment

Students' work is assessed in each area as excellent if they have completed all parts with no errors, skilled if parts are incomplete with three or fewer errors, and needing help if they have not done parts and have more than four errors.

■ Environment Check

This example is provided by Mary Porter and Sharon Neifer. Students work in teams to make observations about the use of air, water, land, or energy. They record their observations in a journal, then write team letters to local newspapers, create posters, create ads for radio and television, and so on. Students then present the various products to the class. The first thing I find particularly interesting about this lesson is that the content focuses on the naturalist intelligence. Second, it requires the use of a number of intelligences. Third, it thematically integrates basic skills and transforming learning to a real-life context. They learn basic information about the environment, then become responsible citizens to do something with the information.

The Activity

Members of teams observe ways their community uses one of four resources—air, water, land, or energy. They keep journals that list ways the resource is being used and wasted. If the resource is air, they look for sources of pollution. If the resource is water, they look for sources of pollution and waste. If the resource is land, they examine the use and misuse of land in the community. If the resource is energy, they look for waste of heat, air conditioning, electricity, and gasoline. They record ways the problems affect them and ways to solve the problems. They meet in their groups to draw a map of their community that shows places where problems in uses of the resource exist. They write a letter to their newspaper in which they report their findings and offer solutions. They produce an ad for radio or television, designed to interest other citizens in the problems they found and to encourage action. They present the map, letter, ad, and any results to the class.

The Assessment

Students' products are evaluated as excellent if they show how the problem affects them, offer solutions, produce an informative map, a letter, and ads. Students are considered skilled if they complete many of the products. Students need help if they don't complete the products.

■ Civil War Extravaganza

This example was provided by Dale Burkholder. It is a fine demonstration of a way to ensure all intelligences are involved and students can tap into them to learn material. Students experience the Civil War in multimodal ways. The assessment does not delineate criteria for various levels of performance.

The Activity

Working individually or in pairs, students complete a project related to a Civil War topic. Each project must include a typed or word processed 5-by-8-inch note card that provides background information and a bibliography card that lists the references used. Students must use a minimum of three resources for individual projects and five resources for partner projects. Only one encyclopedia reference is allowed for each project. Students may not use a history textbook as a resource. They choose a project from the following list:

1. Model (one to two people): scale model of a Civil War person, place, thing, or event; information card must include who, what, where, when, how

2. Cookbook (one person): book of at least ten Civil War era recipes, including soup, main dish, vegetable or side dish, bread, and dessert; information card must include material about diet of Civil War soldiers

3. Board Game (one to two people): playable board game based on Civil War with title, rules and procedures, and a minimum of fifty Civil War facts; information card must contain information related to overall topic of game

The Assessment

Students are assessed on following directions, originality and creativity, accuracy of information, quality, and effort.

Part 3

Some Conclusions

8

Multiple Approaches to MI Rubrics

On Finding Your Pathway _____

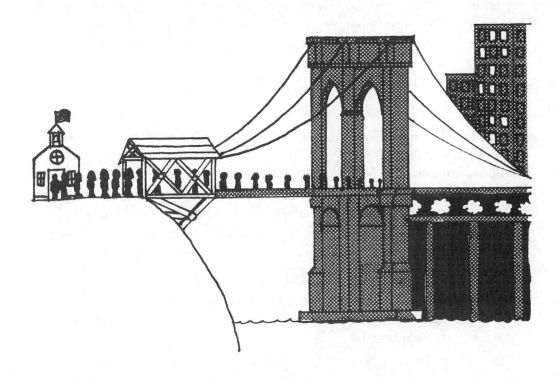

I have no doubt whatever that most people live . . . in a very restricted circle of their potential being. They make use of a very small portion of their possible consciousness . . . much like the person who, out of the whole body organism, should get into the habit of using and moving only the little finger. We all have reservoirs of life to draw upon of which we do not dream.

—William James

In this final chapter I have two main goals. The first is to share a process for using the rubrics that I present in chapters 4 through 6 and a process for creating your own MI-based rubrics. The second is to share several other approaches to creating and using MI rubrics—approaches that view rubrics somewhat differently and suggest different models than those I have presented in this book.

Creating and Using MI Rubrics

In the last three chapters I suggest eighty MI assessment instruments. I describe some two hundred and forty rubrics for evaluating students' MI-based performances using the various instruments. I describe some four hundred and eighty questions for assessing students relative mastery of the content in and through the various intelligence modes. And I present more than thirty-five examples of how teachers are actually using multiple intelligences and MI rubrics in the classroom to assess their students. If you are feeling a bit overwhelmed right now, don't worry, *so am I*!!

This section offers several simple, practical ways to get started and to put it all together. First I share a process for creating MI-based rubrics for any assessment.

Develop Assessment Objectives

Articulate your objectives and anticipated outcomes. Include the following:

- The content to be assessed—specifically, what students are responsible for proving they understand
- The intelligence—specifically, which intelligence skills and capacities you want them to use
- The benefit to students—specifically, how the assessment will deepen, enhance, and expand students' understanding of the required material

Select Assessment Instruments

Turn to the Multiple Intelligence Assessment Menu (page 36) and decide which assessment strategies are in line with your objectives for the assessment. Ask yourself the following questions:

- In how many ways do I need to ask students to represent their understanding of the material to make sure they've really got it?
- Which intelligences and tools shall I use in my teaching that students are relatively comfortable using and that will promote more learning during the assessment itself?
- Which instruments will give me the best picture of students' understanding and are most in line with my overall objectives?

Create the Rubrics

Articulate the criteria by which students' work will be judged and, if necessary, graded. Adapt the rubrics for the assessment instruments you have chosen from the rubrics in chapters 4 through 6. Remember to do the following:

- Clearly state up front exactly what content is and is not covered in the assessment. Articulate what constitutes the various levels of successful understanding; move from merely presenting factual information to synthesis, integration, and transfer.
- Clearly state up front the criteria for the assessment and *provide examples of what a performance might look like for each level*, moving from your adaptations of the *basic* to the *complex* to the *higher order*.

Solicit Student Input and Feedback

Elicit student participation in creating and agreeing on the rubrics. Make sure to ask yourself the following:

- Do students genuinely understand the content and intelligence rubrics?
- Do students feel that the rubrics are fair? Are they confident that they can succeed? Do they feel *positively* challenged?
- What do students want to add or take away from the rubrics? Be willing to make adjustments in the rubric using your overall objective for the assessment as a guideline.

Streamlining the Process

On page 200 is a form you can use to streamline this process. It is also something you can use to get students deeply involved. On page 201 is a form I filled out as if I were assessing my reader's understanding of some of the material in this book.

More MI Approaches to Assessment

In *Multiple Intelligence Approaches to Assessment* (Lazear 1994), I present five approaches to using the MI Assessment Menu. These bear repeating with some rubric-specific comments for each option. I assume the content or curriculum rubrics are already in place. I address only the intelligence rubric.

Eight-in-One Assessments

Basically the goal is to use all the intelligences to assess understanding. You may, on some occasions, select the specific instruments from the menu and, on others, individual students may select them. But the key to this approach is that students must demonstrate their understanding in all eight ways.

Obviously, the overarching rubric in this approach is that students use all eight intelligences, so the specific rubrics must show the levels of performance for all

Multiple Intelligence
Rubrics Planning Work Sheet

Content Objective

Intelligence Objective

CONTENT

What Knowledge?

Rubric Definitions

Basic	Complex	Higher Order

INTELLIGENCES

What Instruments?

Rubric Definitions

Basic	Complex	Higher Order

Multiple Intelligence
Rubrics Planning Work Sheet

Content Objective

to understand the basic elements of MI theory and ways to use the theory to assess students' understanding

Intelligence Objective

to express understanding of MI through a mural or montage, a sound illustration, and an autobiographical report

CONTENT

What Knowledge?

- What the multiple intelligences are
- How to use MI to plan lessons
- How to use MI to assess understanding

Rubric Definitions

Basic	Complex	Higher Order
Can name the eight intelligences	Can name and explain the eight intelligences	Can name, explain, and give examples of eight intelligences
MI as a simple add-on activity to existing lessons	MI used frequently during lesson	MI is fully integrated into teaching process
Traditional test with one MI idea added; not an integral part	An equal balance of MI tasks and traditional testing	Wholly new assessments that assess MI performance and content

INTELLIGENCES

What Instruments?

- Visual-spatial mural or montage
- Musical-rhythmic sound illustrations
- Intrapersonal autobiography

Rubric Definitions

Basic	Complex	Higher Order
Eight images presented that accurately represent MI	Several images for each intelligence that show connections	Images flowing together to present an integrated view of MI
Sounds are very much "the expected" (perhaps borrowed from TV)	Sounds are unusual and reflect unusual connections	Creates an interesting experience of the intelligences
Nothing new here: "I already knew all of this before."	New discoveries and questions about self	New understanding of self; sees several applications

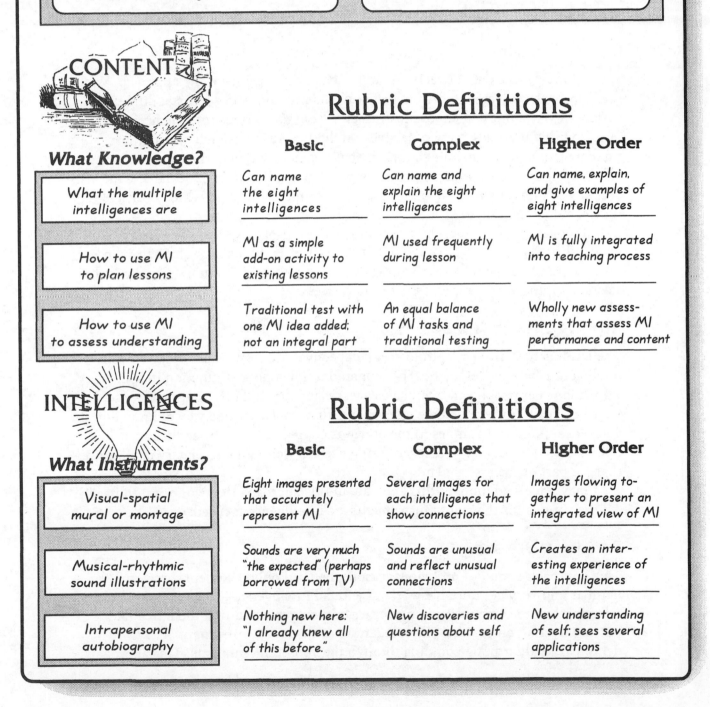

eight. Depending on your objectives for the assessment, you may want to define the rubrics for the individual intelligences as well, especially if the choice of instruments is yours. If you allow students to choose, you could help them create their own rubrics for each instrument they choose. However, it would also be valid to keep the rubrics at a more general level, focused on the actual employment of each intelligence in the performance. In other words, the rubric could be simply that students must use all intelligences to show understanding in any way possible, or it could be more specific (for example, they must draw a picture, do a role-play). In the latter case, depending on the objective of the assessment, you would specify the basic, complex, and higher-order criteria for each product.

Eight Options

Some similarities exist between this approach and the eight-in-one approach. With this approach, you are concerned that students display their understanding in a variety of ways, but you choose instruments from the various intelligences that are in line with your assessment objectives. Individual students then select at least three instruments from your selections that they feel will help them prove their learning and understanding. If students are very familiar and comfortable with MI, you might allow them to choose or create instruments through which they feel they can demonstrate their understanding.

Obviously, if you choose the instruments, you probably have some sense of what rubrics will meet your assessment objectives. If students create their own instruments, they should also, with your guidance, create the rubrics; make sure they are in line with your assessment objectives.

Intelligence Focused

The truth is that, from a neurological perspective, it is impossible to have a one-intelligence-based assessment. The human brain just doesn't function in such a way. In normal people, all intelligences work together in fairly well-orchestrated ways. You can, however, create assessments that *emphasize* one way of knowing. If you reexamine the examples in the previous chapters, you will see that a teacher often states the *primary intelligence* being used as well as the *secondary intelligences* that are part of the assessment.

I may have said more in this book about this approach than you want to hear! All the rubrics for the eighty instruments are intelligence focused.

Random Drawing

This approach should, for obvious reasons, be used only if students are very familiar and very comfortable working with all intelligences. The process involves selecting two to three instruments for each intelligence, putting them in a hat, passing the hat, and asking each student to draw out an instrument. They will demonstrate their understanding through the chosen instruments. This approach is especially useful when you want students to learn how to transfer their supposed learning and understanding to other situations and other contexts.

When you write the instruments on the slips of paper, do so in a way that embodies or suggests the rubric, for example, "Create a dance routine that lasts three to five minutes and demonstrates the growth and development of a plant" or "Create a sculpture that includes various colors, textures, and shapes to show the parts of the living cell." The rubrics that would grow out of these assignments would state how many minutes and how many plant growth stages excellent, good, and undeveloped dances would have, and how many colors and parts of a cell an excellent, good, and undeveloped sculpture would have.

Partners Assessing Partners

Although from the outset this assessment may seem interpersonal, it very quickly moves beyond this intelligence. After being told about the content and assessment objectives, pairs of students discuss how they could best demonstrate their under-standing of the required content. They individually select at least three products from various intelligences that will best show their learning. After hearing comments, individual students use the instruments their partners have chosen to create full assessments, then administer the assessments.

If students have been immersed in MI, they should be able to create rubrics for the various MI performances or products on the menu. However, you must carefully monitor this process to ensure fair and high-level expectations.

I am not suggesting that my list of approaches is exhaustive, nor am I suggesting that mine are even "right" approaches. Myriad creative ways exist to use MI to enhance, deepen, and expand students' learning and understanding. I am simply "priming the pump," so to speak, and in so doing helping you tap your own creative resources.

Neither am I suggesting that my list of various MI assessment instruments is exhaustive. The list represents the best of my thinking at the time of this writing. Please feel free to drastically amend these lists. My only caution is *make sure any new instruments you add are intelligence fair,* that is, couched in the unique way of knowing, the language, the core operations, and the cognitive process of the intelligence.

Other Models for MI Rubrics

Assessment and rubrics are two of the hottest discussion, staff development, conference, and debate topics in education today. Is it any wonder, then, that there are almost as many approaches to assessment and rubrics as there are people involved in the discussion? In this final section, I share several approaches that I find to be quite provocative in my own thinking about fair assessments and the rubrics that will help us create them. The models I present are eclectic, pulled from research and insights from a number of people, schools, books, and districts.

Assessments that Emulate the Masters: Exemplary Performance Rubric

In chapter 2, I mentioned Grant Wiggins's proposal that, if we are concerned with authentic assessments, we should design the academic equivalents of the sports event, the dance recital, the concert, and so on, where *the performance itself is the assessment*. No one would ever suggest that the Green Bay Packers should sit down and take a paper and pencil test to show what they know about football! The exemplary performance rubric helps us move assessment in this direction.

In the mid 1980s, Project Zero at Harvard University, in collaboration with the Educational Testing Service and Pittsburgh Public Schools, launched a program called Arts Propel. Arts Propel could be described as an experimental arts education program designed to expose students to ways of thinking exhibited by individuals involved in the arts themselves. The Exemplary Performance Rubric is based on an assessment process called "domain projects," which was designed for Arts Propel. Zeffoules et al. (n.d.) describe domain projects:

> Domain projects can be briefly described as sets of integrated exercises designed to convey a concept or dimension central to an artistic domain. Administered over several class periods, these exercises approach the concept from a variety of angles, encourage problem-finding as well as problem-solving . . . It should be stressed that domain projects are not themselves curricula or even curricular guidelines; rather they are flexible models which can be adapted by teachers for specific classrooms, teaching styles, and curricular goals. (10)

The key is to expose students to exemplary performances such as dramas, comedy routines, or dances, so the students get an image of what is involved in a fine performance. Then students demonstrate their knowledge of particular concepts through dramas, comedy sequences, or dances in which they emulate and incorporate as many of the qualities of the exemplary performance as possible.

In *Multiple Intelligence Approaches to Assessment* (Lazear 1994) I include a number of examples of these curricular performances—a living historical museum, a math olympics competition, a cultural immersion festival, a hands-on health fair, and others.

Assessments that Develop Talents and Skills: Task Performance Rubrics

In some ways the Task Performance Rubric is similar to the MI Performance Rubrics in chapters 4 through 6. The main difference I see is that the task performance rubric is wholly linked to and defined by specific performance criteria whereas the MI rubrics are related to intelligence capacity building and the development of high levels of intelligence-specific cognitive processes.

The key to this rubric is the clear delineation of the boundaries for a successful performance of a particular assessment task. We already clearly delineate criteria when we assign written work. We will say such things as "Your report must be five hundred words long, it must be typed or word processed, you must cite at least five references to support the thesis of your paper . . . " With this rubric, we simply do the same thing for any specific assessment task.

A value of this approach is that it allows you to create a cognitive complexity in the execution of the task that will often genuinely challenge students to higher-level performances and to more in-depth presentations of their learning. A danger is that you might simply create a string of alternative, enjoyable activities that do little more than momentarily overcome boredom. Creating truly effective assessment tasks that promote and deepen student learning is more than just reaching into a kit bag of fun activities. ASCD *Education Update* (1995a) observes,

> Creating effective assessment tasks requires thinking through curriculum content to establish learning outcomes, then designing performance activities that will allow students to demonstrate their achievement of those outcomes, and specifying criteria by which they will be evaluated . . .

> To develop meaningful performance assessment tasks that will reveal the learning that teachers hope to seed, educators need to take an assessment perspective from the beginning . . . *"If you think like an assessor, you're thinking, 'Given what I want them to learn, what counts as evidence that they understand that?'" [Grant Wiggins] says. "That's a very different question than 'What is a good activity?'"* (1, 6; emphasis mine)

Assessments that Promote Real World Problem Solving: Special Project Rubrics

A number of teachers' examples in this book provide excellent examples of the special project rubric. The essence of this model is thinking through all of the aspects of a project and creating for each specific rubrics that challenge students to perform at high levels. Campbell, Campbell, and Dickinson (1992) note the importance of project-based learning:

> Open-ended in nature, a project poses multiple solutions and engages students in a "whole" situation, one that encourages discovery of its parts, relationships, meaning, and resolution. Projects can have strong academic value when based upon concepts, principles, and skills central to a whole body of knowledge and skill. Through immersion in a project, students are personally and actively involved in their learning, they develop and use a wide range of intelligences, and they find excitement in connecting schooling with real life. (197)

Following are a possible set of rubrics you could use for this model. Each could be scored on the 4-point scales represented, and of course, you could include additional aspects or omit some included here.

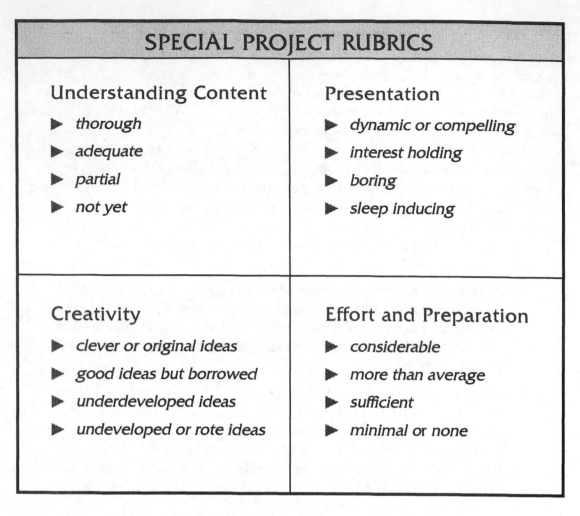

SPECIAL PROJECT RUBRICS

Understanding Content

▶ *thorough*

▶ *adequate*

▶ *partial*

▶ *not yet*

Presentation

▶ *dynamic or compelling*

▶ *interest holding*

▶ *boring*

▶ *sleep inducing*

Creativity

▶ *clever or original ideas*

▶ *good ideas but borrowed*

▶ *underdeveloped ideas*

▶ *undeveloped or rote ideas*

Effort and Preparation

▶ *considerable*

▶ *more than average*

▶ *sufficient*

▶ *minimal or none*

Assessments that Show Work *and* How One Works: Portfolios and "Process-folios"

I discuss portfolios and "process-folios" in chapter 3 of *Multiple Intelligence Approaches to Assessment* (1994); I revisit these models here to consider rubrics.

Portfolios

Hamm and Adams (1991) describe a portfolio as "more than a folder of student work; it is a deliberate, specific collection of accomplishments" (20). Vavrus (1990) adds, "A portfolio is more than just a container of stuff. It's a systematic and organized collection of evidence used by the teacher and student to monitor growth of the student's knowledge, skills, and attitudes in a specific subject area" (48). Almost anything that gives evidence of students' learning can be included in a portfolio, including (but not limited to) journal or log entries or any self-reflection, exemplary products, photographs, videotapes of performances, audiocassettes, and so on. Although no single object in the portfolio tells the whole story, the composite should give an accurate and somewhat comprehensive picture of where a given student is.

What about using portfolios in assessment? ASCD *Education Update* (1995b) states the following about the power of using portfolios to assess learning:

> Portfolios allow students to assume ownership in ways that few other instructional approaches allow. Portfolio assessment requires students to collect and reflect on examples of their work . . . If carefully assembled, portfolios become an intersection of instruction and assessment: they are not just instruction or assessment but, rather, both. Together, instruction and assessment give more than either gives separately. (61)

What are some possibilities for using portfolios? The following list is based on the work of Kay Burke (1993).

- Teachers could assign formative grades based on specific content and intelligence rubrics to each piece of work.
- Teachers could give a summative grade to the entire portfolio; the grade would be derived from teacher- and student-developed rubrics.
- Parents, teacher, and student could focus on the portfolio in a conference.
- Teachers and students could focus on the portfolio to set academic goals and determine areas that need work.
- Teachers could pass selected portfolio pieces to successive teachers so that students would have clear pictures of their accomplishments.
- Teachers could have a series of intelligence-specific portfolios to document growth and development in the respective intelligences.
- Students could use an ungraded portfolio to reflect on their growth and development, and teachers could use it to reflect on their effectiveness.

This list could obviously go on and on, and you should probably expand it a great deal to maximize the use of this very powerful assessment tool. As with everything else we have discussed in this book, the key to turning portfolios into a viable and valid assessment instrument is creating the rubrics by which they will be evaluated.

"Process-folios"

In his article "Zero-Based Arts Education: An Introduction to ARTS PROPEL," Gardner explains the difference between a portfolio and a process-folio:

> We have also introduced a second educational vehicle—the portfolio (which I sometimes called the "process-folio"). Most artists' portfolios contain only the very best works by an artist, the set by which the artist would wish to be judged in a competition. In contrast our [process-folios] are much more like "works in progress." In their [process-folios], students include not just finished works but also original sketches, interim drafts, critiques by themselves and others, art works by others they admire or dislike and which bear in some

way on the current project. Students are sometimes asked to present the whole folder of materials; at other times they are asked to select out those pieces which appear particularly informative or pivotal in their own development. (80)

Many of the options listed for using portfolios in assessment can also be used with processfolios; however the focus shifts from a more or less finished product to the dynamic, creative process that leads to a product. Thus the rubrics for evaluating a processfolio would be much more fluid, dynamic, and integral to the ebb and flow of the creative process. Following are some guidelines based on "A Better Balance: ARTS PROPEL as an Alternative to Discipline-Based Arts Education":

- Look for students' ability to take risks, to try new things, start over if they are not satisfied with their work.

- Watch for the process of how students develop ideas, pursue serious or difficult work over time; look for their capacity to edit and revise their work, to seek and try alternative solutions.

- Examine students' capacity to build on their own and others' past knowledge.

- Look for an appreciation and understanding of their creative processes and abilities.

- Examine ways in which students value the processes that lead to a final product.

Not only do processfolios profoundly benefit students because they directly promote lifelong learning, they also provide teachers and administrators with a rare and invaluable glimpse into students' developmental journeys. Processfolios provide tangible evidence of students' movement across a variety of cognitive and intelligence levels from novice to expert. In Zeffoules (n.d.) a "special needs" student, articulates the benefits of an Arts Propel–style processfolio: "You get to look back and see where your strengths and weaknesses are, and you can see the whole picture. [Process-folios] make you get more involved in your work, develop it. You take your time more. I also like [group discussions] a lot. Now when I'm going to do art work, I find I ask myself questions all the time. And when I go to a museum, I know why people stand in front of a painting, and I look for what the artist is trying to achieve, and what he's trying to express; for texture, colors, and how the picture fits" (9).

My goal in this last section has been to underscore the necessity of creating MI-based rubrics; in fact, we must do so if we are to ask the tax-paying public to understand and support this way of teaching and learning. It is no more or less difficult to use all intelligences in instruction and assessment than it is to use the two that are currently the focus of more than 95 percent of our approaches to assessment. If the rubrics are in place, the assessment data we receive are at least as valid as the information we receive on current verbal-linguistic and logical-mathematical assessments. The MI approach to assessment and rubrics gives us a much more accurate and fair picture of students' academic progress.

Epilogue

As I mentioned, last year I was privileged to conduct several workshops and speak at a major conference in Australia and New Zealand. In a workshop in New Zealand, I was given a copy of the "Principles of Assessment for Better Learning" taken from the New Zealand Department of Education (1989). In this concluding section I return to where I began, namely, trying to paint a picture of a new future for education today. The most encouraging and exciting thing about my venture is that it is already coming to be; often in a "one-step-forward, two-steps-back" fashion, nonetheless it is happening.

I use nine principles from the New Zealand document to guide my thinking. For each point of these principles I provide a checklist of practical benchmarks or things to look for that are possible indicators that "the new is upon us."

The interests of students shall be paramount. Assessment shall be planned and implemented in ways that maximize benefits for students while minimizing any negative effects on them.

- Do assessment practices enhance, deepen, and expand students' learning?
- Is assessment at one with the teaching and learning process (as opposed to something apart that occurs after the teaching on some other day)?
- Do students understand the assessment process and are they involved in creating how it will happen so it is a partnership (as opposed to "teacher's secret" and something that is done *to* students)?

The primary purpose of assessment shall be to provide information that can be used to identify strengths and to guide improvement.

- Do grading and scoring practices give students positive feedback that can help them improve?
- Do our assessments celebrate students' learning and achievement (as opposed to focusing on their failure or what they don't know)?
- Do we use assessment information in prescriptive ways that create opportunities for guaranteeing *every* student's success (as opposed to being content with the normal curve that says some will succeed, some will not, and most will be average)?

Assessment information should not be used for judgmental or political purposes if such use would be likely to cause harm to students or to the effectiveness of teachers in schools.

- Are we promoting high standards through assessment by seeking genuine student understanding (as opposed to low-level information recall)?

- Are we involved in promoting the use of scores as positive feedback for improving our schools (as opposed to unthinking practice of publishing school test scores in local newspapers with little or no understanding of what the scores *actually* mean)?

- Are we getting understandable information into the hands of school board members and other elected officials regarding "what's best for kids" (as opposed to wringing our hands over bad policies)?

Every effort should be made to ensure that assessment and evaluation procedures are fair to all.

- Are students given many options to use their many "ways of knowing" to demonstrate their understanding of required material (as opposed to the idea that the ultimate and only true test of their knowledge is a paper-and-pencil assessment)?

- Are students actively involved in understanding the assessment process and do they participate in creating the ways in which they will be assessed (as opposed to a teacher-driven assessment process as something we do *to* students)?

- Are students encouraged to ask questions about the assessment if they do not understand and are they required to discuss and defend their answers in a performance (as opposed to taking answers at face value or assuming there is only one right answer)?

Community involvement is essential to the credibility and impact of assessment and evaluation processes.

- Are there "assessment literacy" programs that are helping the public understand the assessment process and become "informed consumers" of assessment data and information they receive (as opposed to simply accepting test scores at face value with little or no questioning of their meaning)?

- Do we use parent-teacher conferences as occasions to educate the public about current brain research and how it is being applied in education today (as opposed to a simple report on "your child's progress" or dealing with problems)?

- Are there forums where educators and the general public can interact, ask questions, and build consensus on what our schools should be (as opposed to being in separate camps with battle lines drawn between them)?

Careful consideration should be given to the motivational effects of assessment and evaluation practices.

- Is assessment viewed as an exciting opportunity for students to demonstrate what they know and what they can do (as opposed to being an occasion of fear, anxiety, and stress)?

- Is assessment being used to positively challenge students (as opposed to threatening them with bad grades or loss of certain privileges if they don't do well)?

- Are we using assessments to intrinsically motivate students' to be lifelong learners and to have a love of learning itself (as opposed to the extrinsic "you better do well on this test or else!")?

In the assessment of intellectual outcomes, substantial attention should be devoted to more sophisticated skills such as understanding of principles, applying skill and knowledge to new tasks, and investigating, analyzing, and discussing complex issues and problems.

- Do our assessments require high-level performances of understanding (as opposed to low-level regurgitation of memorized facts)?

- Do our assessments promote the development and growth of students' cognitive abilities in all intelligence areas (as opposed to the mere ability to write or calculate the so-called right answer)?

- Do our assessments occur in or simulate "in context" (real life) applications and transfer of learning (as opposed to a knowledge of a series of disembodied, unconnected facts, figures, dates, processes, and so on)?

Emphasis should be given to identifying and reporting educational progress and growth, rather than to a comparison of individuals or schools.

- Do we use progress reports to help students improve (as opposed to ranking students in individual classes or in the whole school)?

- Do we report on students' educational progress in ways that open the future and indicate areas of continued growth for the students (as opposed to labeling students with various letter or number grades)?

- Do the reports sent home to parents provide a holistic picture of students' educational journey and development (as opposed to simply reporting on the three Rs)?

The choices made in reporting assessment information largely determine the benefit or harm resulting from the information. For this reason, the selection, presentation, and discussion of information must be controlled by the principles outlined previously.

In my opinion, this concluding principle stands on its own and needs no further elaboration from me. However, if we in fact allowed the above principles to control the selection and presentation of assessment and assessment information, we would indeed move into what has been my vision in this book: *a brain-based, intelligence-fair approach to assessment.*

Appendix
National Education Goals

From the National Education Goals Panel
125 22nd Street, NW, Suite 502
Washington, DC 20037
(202) 724-0015
Fax: (202) 632-0957
Web: http://www.negp.gov
E-mail: NEGP@goalline.org

Goal 1: Ready to Learn

By the year 2000, all children in America will start school ready to learn.

Goal 2: School Completion

By the year 2000, the high school graduation rate will increase to at least 90 percent.

Goal 3: Student Achievement and Citizenship

By the year 2000, all students will leave grades 4, 8, and 12 having demonstrated competency over challenging subject matter including English, mathematics, science, foreign languages, civics and government, economics, arts, history, and geography, and every school in America will ensure that all students learn to use their minds well, so they may be prepared for responsible citizenship, further learning, and productive employment in our nation's modern economy.

Goal 4: Teacher Education and Professional Development

By the year 2000, the nation's teaching force will have access to programs for the continued improvement of their professional skills and the opportunity to acquire the knowledge and skills needed to instruct and prepare all American students for the next century.

Goal 5: Mathematics and Science

By the year 2000, United States students will be first in the world in mathematics and science achievement.

Goal 6: Adult Literacy and Lifelong Learning

By the year 2000, every adult American will be literate and will possess the knowledge and skills necessary to compete in a global economy and exercise the rights and responsibilities of citizenship.

Goal 7: Safe, Disciplined, and Alcohol- and Drug-free Schools

By the year 2000, every school in the United States will be free of drugs, violence, and the unauthorized presence of firearms and alcohol and will offer a disciplined environment conducive to learning.

Goal 8: Parental Participation

By the year 2000, every school will promote partnerships that will increase parental involvement and participation in promoting the social, emotional, and academic growth of children.

Bibliography

Alverno College Faculty. 1985. *Assessment at Alverno College,* rev. ed. Milwaukee, Wis.: Alverno College.

Archibald, D. A., and F. Newmann. 1988. *Beyond Standardized Testing: Assessing Authentic Academic Achievement in the Secondary School.* Reston, Va.: National Association of Secondary School Principals.

Armstrong, T. 1987. *In Their Own Way: Discovering and Encouraging Your Child's Own Personal Learning Style.* Los Angeles: J. P. Tarcher.

———. 1993. *7 Kinds of Smart: Identifying and Developing Your Many Intelligences.* New York: Penguin.

Association for Supervision and Curriculum Development. 1995a. "Designing Performance Assessment Tasks." *Education Update* 37, 6.

———. 1995b. "Using Assessment to Motivate Students." *Education Update* 37, 6.

Bellanca, J., C. Chapman, and B. Swartz. 1994. *Multiple Assessments for Multiple Intelligences.* Palatine, Ill.: Skylight.

Bloom, B. 1956. *Taxonomy of Educational Objectives.* New York: David McKay.

Bloom, B., G. Madaus, and J. T. Hastings. 1981. *Evaluation to Improve Learning.* New York: McGraw-Hill.

Boggeman, S., T. Hoerr, and C. Wallach. 1996. *Succeeding with Multiple Intelligences: Teaching through the Personal Intelligences.* St. Louis, Mo.: The New City School.

Brandt, R. 1992. "On Performance Assessment: A Conversation with Grant Wiggins." *Educational Leadership* 49, 8: 35–37.

Burke, K. 1993. *How to Assess Thoughtful Outcomes.* Palatine, Ill.: IRI, Skylight.

Caine, G., R. N. Caine, and S. Crowell. 1994. *MindShifts: A Brain-Based Process for Restructuring Schools and Renewing Education.* Tucson, Ariz.: Zephyr Press.

Caine, R., and G. Caine. 1990. "Understanding a Brain-Based Approach to Learning and Teaching." *Educational Leadership* 48, 2: 66–70.

———. 1991. *Making Connections: Teaching and the Human Brain.* Alexandria, Va.: ASCD.

Campbell, B. 1994. *The Multiple Intelligences Handbook: Lesson Plans and More.* Stanwood, Wash.: Campbell.

Campbell, L., B. Campbell, and D. Dickinson. 1992. *Teaching and Learning through Multiple Intelligences.* Seattle: New Horizons for Learning.

Costa, A., and B. Kalick. 1992. "Reassessing Assessment." In *If Minds Matter: A Foreword to the Future.* vol. 2. Palatine, Ill.: IRI, Skylight. 275–80.

Department of Education and Science. 1988. *National Curriculum: Task Group on Assessment and Testing.* Great Britain.

Dickinson, D., ed. 1991. *Creating the Future: Perspectives on Educational Change.* Aston Cling, Bucks, U.K.: Accelerated Learning Systems.

———. 1992a. "Technology and the Multiple Intelligences." *Intelligence Connections* 1, 2, and 3.

———. 1992b. "Learning for Life." In *If Minds Matter: A Foreword to the Future,* vol. 1. Pallatine, Ill,: IRI, Skylight. 51–61.

Diez, M. E., and C. J. Moon. 1992. "What Do We Want Students to Know? . . . and Other Important Questions." *Educational Leadership* 49, 8: 38–41.

Faculty of The New City School. 1994. *Celebrating Multiple Intelligences: Teaching for Success.* St. Louis, Mo.: The New City School.

Feuerstein, R. 1980. *Instrumental Enrichment: An Intervention Program for Cognitive Modifiability.* Baltimore, Md.: University Park Press.

Gardner, H. 1982. *Developmental Psychology: An Introduction.* Boston: Little, Brown.

———. 1983. *Frames of Mind: The Theory of Multiple Intelligences.* New York: Basic.

———. 1987. "Developing the Spectrum of Human Intelligences: Teaching in the Eighties, a Need to Change." *Harvard Educational Review* 57: 87–93.

———. 1991. *The Unschooled Mind: How Children Think and How Schools Should Teach.* New York: Basic.

———. 1993. *Multiple Intelligences: The Theory in Practice.* New York: Basic.

———. 1996. "Are There Additional Intelligences? The Case for Naturalist, Spiritual, and Existential Intelligences." Cambridge, Mass.: Harvard Project Zero.

———. 1997. "Zero-based Arts Education: An Introduction to ARTS PROPEL." Cambridge, Mass.: Harvard Project Zero.

Glasser, W. 1986. *Control Theory in the Classroom.* New York: Perennial Library.

Glickman, C. 1991. "Pretending Not to Know What We Know." *Educational Leadership* 48, 8: 4–9.

Gorman, B., and W. Johnson. 1991. *Successful Schooling for Everyone.* Bloomington, Ind.: National Education Services.

Grady, E. 1992. *The Portfolio Approach to Assessment.* Bloomington, Ind.: Phi Delta Kappa Educational Foundation.

Guilford, J. 1988. *Way beyond I.Q.* Buffalo, N.Y.: Creative Education Foundation.

Hamm, M., and D. Adams. 1991. "Portfolio: It's Not Just for Artists Anymore." *The Science Teacher.* May: 18–21.

Harman, W. 1988. *The Global Mind Change: The Promise of the Last Years of the Twentieth Century.* Indianapolis, Ind.: Knowledge Systems.

Harman, W., and H. Rheingold. 1985. *Higher Creativity: Liberating the Unconscious for Breakthrough Insights.* Los Angeles: J. P. Tarcher.

Hart, L. 1983. *Human Brain and Human Learning.* Village of Oak Creek, Ariz.: Books for Educators.

Herman, J. L. 1992. "What Research Tells Us about Good Assessment." *Educational Leadership* 49, 8: 74–78.

Herman, J. L., P. R. Aschbacher, and L. Winters. 1992. *A Practical Guide to Alternative Assessment.* Alexandria, Va.: ASCD.

Jensen, E. 1995. *Brain-Based Learning and Teaching*. Del Mar, Calif.: Turning Point.

Kalick, B. 1989. *Changing Schools into Communities for Thinking*. Grand Forks, N.D.: University of North Dakota Press.

Kohn, A. 1993. *Punished by Rewards: The Trouble with Gold Stars, Incentive Plans, Praise, and Other Bribes*. Boston: Houghton Mifflin.

Kovalick, S. 1993. *ITI: The Model*. Village of Oak Creek, Ariz.: Susan Kovalick.

Lazear, David. 1992. *Teaching for Multiple Intelligences*. Bloomington, Ind.: Phi Delta Kappa Educational Foundation.

———. 1994. *Multiple Intelligence Approaches to Assessment*. Tucson, Ariz.: Zephyr Press.

———. 1997a. *Intelligence Builders for Every Student*. Tucson, Ariz.: Zephyr Press.

———. 1997b. Step beyond Your Limits series. Tucson, Ariz.: Zephyr Press.

———. 1999a. *Eight Ways of Knowing: Teaching for Multiple Intelligences*. Arlington Heights, Ill.: IRI, Skylight.

———. 1999b. *Eight Ways of Teaching: The Artistry of Teaching with Multiple Intelligences*. Arlington Heights, Ill.: IRI, Skylight.

———. 2000. *Pathways of Learning: Teaching Students and Parents about Multiple Intelligences*. Tucson, Ariz.: Zephyr Press.

Majoy, P. 1993. *Doorways to Learning: A Model for Developing the Brain's Full Potential*. Tucson, Ariz.: Zephyr Press.

Meyer, C. 1992. "What's the Difference between Authentic and Performance Assessment?" *Educational Leadership* 49, 8: 39–40.

Mitchell, R. 1992. *Testing for Learning: How New Approaches to Evaluation Can Improve American Schools*. New York: The Free Press.

National Education Goals Panel. 1997. *The National Education Goals Report Summary 1997: Mathematics and Science Achievement for the Twenty-First Century*. Washington, D.C.: NEGP

New Zealand Department of Education. 1989. *Assessment for Better learning: A Public Discussion Document*. Wellington, New Zealand: Department of Education.

Nuttall, D. L. 1992. "Performance Assessment: The Message from England." *Educational Leadership* 49, 8: 45–57.

Oakes, J. 1985. *Keeping Track: How Schools Structure Inequality*. New Haven, Conn.: Yale University Press.

O'Neil, J. 1992. "Putting Performance Assessment to the Test." *Educational Leadership* 49, 8: 14–19.

Perrone, V. 1991. *Expanding Student Assessment*. Alexandria, Va.: ASCD.

Piaget, J. 1972. *The Psychology of Intelligence*. Totowa, N.J.: Littlefield Adams.

Schlechty, P. 1990. *Schools for the 21st Century*. San Francisco: Jossey-Bass.

Stefonek, T. 1991. *Alternative Assessment: A National Perspective*. Oak Brook, Ill.: North Central Regional Educational Laboratory.

Sternberg, R. 1984a. "How Can We Teach Intelligence?" *Educational Leadership* 42, 1: 38–48.

————. 1984b. *Beyond I.Q.: A Triarchic Theory of Human Intelligence*. New York: Cambridge University Press.

————. 1986. *Intelligence Applied: Understanding and Increasing Your Intellectual Skills*. San Diego: Harcourt Brace Jovanovich.

————. 1991. "Thinking Styles: Keys to Understanding Student Performance." *Inquiry: Critical Thinking across the Disciplines* 7, 3: 1, 32–38.

Stiggins, R. 1987. "Design and Development of Performance Assessments." In *Educational Measurement: Issues and Practices*. National Council on Measurement in Education.

————. 1988. "Revitalizing Classroom Assessment." *Phi Delta Kappan* 70, 4.

————. 1991. "Assessment Literacy." *Phi Delta Kappan* 72, 7: 534–39.

Stiggins, R., E. Rubel, and E. Quellmalz. 1986. *Measuring Thinking Skills in the Classroom: A Teacher's Guide*. Portland, Ore.: Northwest Regional Laboratory.

Sylwester, R. 1995. *A Celebration of Neurons: An Educator's Guide to the Human Brain*. Alexandria, Va.: ASCD.

Ulrey, D., and J. Ulrey. 1992. "Developmentally Appropriate Practices Meet Multiple Intelligences." *Intelligences Connections* 2, 1: 4–6.

Wiggins, G. 1988. "Rational Numbers: Toward Grading and Scoring that Helps Rather than Harms Learning." Alexandria, Va.: Coalition of Essential Schools.

————. 1989a. "Teaching to the (Authentic) Test." *Educational Leadership* 46, 7: 41–47.

————. 1989b. "A True Test: Toward More Authentic and Equitable Assessment." *Phi Delta Kappan* 70, 9: 703–13.

————. 1991. "Standards, Not Standardization? Evoking Quality Student Work." *Educational Leadership* 48, 5: 18–25.

————. 1992. "Creating Tests Worth Taking." *Educational Leadership* 49, 8: 26–33.

————. 1997. "Practicing What We Preach in Designing Authentic Assessments." *Educational Leadership* 54, 4: 18–26.

Wolf, D. P., P. G. LeMahieu, and J. Eresh. 1992. "Good Measure: Assessment as a Tool for Educational Reform." *Educational Leadership* 49, 8: 8–13.

Worthen, B. R. 1993. "Critical Issues That Will Determine the future of Alternative Assessment." *Phi Delta Kappan* 74, 6: 444–56.

Worthen, B. R., and J. Sanders. 1987. *Educational Evaluation: Alternative Approaches and Practical Guidelines*. White Plains, N.Y.: Longman.

Zeffoules, R., D. P. Wolf, and H. Gardner. n.d. "A Better Balance: Arts Propel as an Alternative to Discipline-Based Arts Education." unpubl. paper.